Supplement for Beginning Algebra

Arithmetic Review and Algebra Practice

Second Edition

Michele Satty Gage

Frank J. Gelbwasser

New York City Technical College
of the City University of New York

McGraw-Hill, Inc.
College Custom Series

New York St. Louis San Francisco Auckland Bogotá
Caracas Lisbon London Madrid Mexico Milan Montreal
New Delhi Paris San Juan Singapore Sydney Tokyo Toronto

McGraw-Hill's College Custom Series consists of products that are produced from camera-ready copy. Peer review, class testing, and accuracy are primarily the responsibility of the author(s).

SUPPLEMENT FOR BEGINNING ALGEBRA
Arithmetic Review and Algebra Practice

3 4 5 6 7 8 9 0 HAM HAM 9 0 9 8 7 6

ISBN 0-07-022807-8

Editor: Richard G. Klein
Cover Design: Dominic Tinio
Printer/Binder: Hamco Corporation

Preface

Over years of teaching courses in elementary algebra reviewing and reinforcing arithmetic skills, we tried many different textbooks. We found that some books had a lot to offer, but no one book had everything we needed. We supplemented textbooks with hand outs, practice sheets, and practice tests. This provided the students with a customized text, but placed a burden on us every semester to reproduce and distribute numerous materials.

It was our intent to begin with an excellent textbook that covered all the necessary algebra topics and to create a single supplement that met our students' needs:

(1) to help prepare the student for future mathematics courses by providing a selective arithmetic review and additional algebra practice.

(2) to help prepare the student for a Basic Skills Exam.

Experience has shown us that many developmental students enter college with some prior knowledge of arithmetic. However, much of this has been forgotten and a review is essential. This supplement attempts to provide such a review by presenting step-by-step procedures, carefully selected worked out sample exercises and abundant practice. Additionally, sample basic skills exams with comprehensive solutions and textbook references are provided.

> Michele Satty Gage
> Frank J. Gelbwasser

Acknowledgments

I want to thank my husband Tim and son Zachary for keeping each other busy, giving me time to work on this book.

> M.S.G.

A special thanks to my wife Rhonda and my children Alanna, Lara and Kimberly for their unending patience and understanding

> F.J.G.

For this revised edition, a large thanks to our colleagues who have used the book and made suggestions for changes, especially Charles Bernet, Thomas Buckley, Peter Deraney, Jane Rosen and Rhona Noll. More thanks go to Pam Gordon, Margaret Hollander and Betty Whitford at McGraw Hill.

> M.S.G & F.J.G.

CONTENTS

1. Additional Arithmetic Review

WHOLE NUMBERS

Place Value

To determine the place value of a given digit: The location of a digit determines its place value. Put one digit in each column of the place value chart below. The last digit in the number should be all the way to the right. Any empty columns should be on the left.

Place Value Chart

Group:	Billions			Millions			Thousands			Ones		
	one billion	hundred million	ten million	one million	hundred thousand	ten thousand	one thousand	hundred	ten	one

Example 1

Determine the place value of each digit in 5,907.
Place the digits on the chart.

Group:	Billions			Millions			Thousands			Ones		
	one billion	hundred million	ten million	one million	hundred thousand	ten thousand	one thousand	hundred	ten	one
							5	9	0	7

The 5 is in the thousands place.
The 9 is in the hundreds place.
The 0 is in the tens place.
The 7 is in the ones place.

Example 2

Determine the place value of the 6 in the number 45,608,002.
Place the digits on the chart.

Group:	Billions			Millions			Thousands			Ones		
	one billion	hundred million	ten million	one million	hundred thousand	ten thousand	one thousand	hundred	ten	one

$$4\quad 5,\quad 6\quad 0\quad 8,\quad 0\quad 0\quad 2$$

The 6 is in the hundred thousands place.

***To read whole numbers*: Line up the digits on the place value chart. Read each group as if it were a three-digit number, then say the group name. Omit the group name on ones.**

Example 3

Express in words: 9,235,802,501
Place the digits on the chart.

Group:	Billions			Millions			Thousands			Ones		
	one billion	hundred million	ten million	one million	hundred thousand	ten thousand	one thousand	hundred	ten	one

$$9,\quad 2\quad 3\quad 5,\quad 8\quad 0\quad 2,\quad 5\quad 0\quad 1$$

Nine billion, two hundred thirty five million, eight hundred two thousand, five hundred one.

Example 4

Express in words: 50,003,094

Fifty million, three thousand, ninety four.

To write a number: **Line up the digits on the place value chart. Each group but the first must contain exactly three digits. The first group can have 1, 2 or 3 digits. Put zeros in all spaces without digits.**

Example 5

Write two thousand, five hundred sixteen using digits.

Group:	Billions			Millions			Thousands			Ones		
	one billion	hundred million	ten million	one million	hundred thousand	ten thousand	one thousand	hundred	ten	one
							2,	5	1	6

Example 6

Write fifty thousand, three using digits.

50,003

To round a number to a given place:

1. If the first digit to the right of the given place is 5 or greater, add 1 to the digit in the given place.
2. All digits to the right of the given place become zeros.

Example 7

Round 43,567 to the nearest thousand.

44,000

The 3 is in the given place, thousands. Since the first digit to the right of 3 is 5, add 1 to 3.

567 becomes 000.

Example 8

Round 126,908 to the nearest hundred.

126,900

The 9 is in the given place, hundreds. Since the first digit to the right of 9 is not 5 or greater, do not add 1.

Digits to the right of the 9 become zeros.

Adding Whole Numbers

Numbers being added are called addends. The result when you add is the sum or total.

To *add whole numbers:* Line up the numbers vertically with numbers having the same place value in columns. Then add starting with the ones column and work to the left.

<u>Example 9</u>

Find the sum of 45,223 + 76 + 3,502

```
 45,223
     76
  3,502
 ------
 48,801
```

If the total is greater than 9 in any column, remember to carry the excess to the next place on the left.

Subtracting Whole Numbers

The answer when you subtract is called the difference.

To subtract whole numbers: **Line up the numbers vertically with numbers having the same place value in columns. Place the larger number on top. Then subtract starting with the ones column and work to the left.**

<u>Example 10</u>

Find the difference: 158 - 27

```
 158
 -27
 ---
 131
```

<u>Example 11</u>

Subtract 438 from 5062.

```
 5062
 -438
 ----
 4624
```

Since you cannot take 8 away from 2, borrow 1 from the 6 to get 12. The 6 becomes a 5. Then subtract 8 from 12. You will also have to borrow from the 5.

Estimating Sums and Differences

To estimate sums and differences by rounding: **Round each number to the first place. Then compute an estimated answer.**

Example 12

Estimate the sum: 56,987 + 2,056 + 18,031

$$
\begin{array}{r}
60,000 \\
2,000 \\
+\underline{20,000} \\
82,000
\end{array}
$$

Round 56,987 to 60,000
Round 2,056 to 2,000
Round 18,031 to 20,000

Example 13

Estimate the difference: 569,234 - 90,803

$$
\begin{array}{r}
600,000 \\
-\underline{90,000} \\
510,000
\end{array}
$$

Multiplying Whole Numbers

The numbers being multiplied are called factors. The result when you multiply is called the product.

To multiply whole numbers: **Line up the numbers vertically, with numbers having the same place value in columns. Then multiply digit by digit, preserving place value.**

Example 14

Multiply 28 x 57

$$
\begin{array}{r}
28 \\
\times \underline{57} \\
196 \\
\underline{140} \\
1596
\end{array}
$$

The last digit of each product goes under the digit doing the multiplying.

To multiply when numbers end in zeros: **Multiply the numbers omitting the zeros at the end. Then attach the total number of ending zeros in the factors to the product.**

Example 15
6000 x 300

   1,800,000

Multiply 6 x 3 = 18
Attach five zeros to the 18.

Example 16
35,000,000 x 14,000

Attach 9 zeros to the product of 35 x 14

```
          35
         x14
         140
         35_
         490
```
490,000,000,000

To estimate the product by rounding:

Method 1: Round each factor to the first place. Then calculate using the method for multiplying numbers ending with zeros.
(Note: If you have rounded both factors up, the number will be too large. If you have rounded both factors down, the number will be too small.)

Method 2: If you want a more accurate estimate, round one factor up, the other factor down.

Example 17

Estimate the product of 34,567 x 521

```
        30,000
       x  500
    15,000,000
```

This is an illustration of Method 1. Since both factors were rounded down, the product is too small.

Long Division

Division may be written $a \div b$ or $\dfrac{a}{b}$ or $b\overline{)a}$ where b is the divisor and a is the dividend. The answer when you divide is called the quotient. The steps in long division are:

- divide
- multiply
- subtract
- compare
- bring down

Example 18

Divide 355 by 5

$$
\begin{array}{r}
71 \\
5\overline{)355} \\
-35 \\
\hline
5 \\
-5 \\
\hline
\end{array}
$$

Example 19

$3,536 \div 17$

$$
\begin{array}{r}
208 \\
17\overline{)3536} \\
-34 \\
\hline
136 \\
-136 \\
\hline
\end{array}
$$

Example 20
Divide 238 by 15

$$
\begin{array}{r}
16R8 \\
15\overline{)238} \\
-15 \\
\hline
88 \\
-80 \\
\hline
8
\end{array}
$$

To estimate division by rounding:

Method 1: Round the divisor and the dividend to the first place. Then divide.
Method 2: If you want a more accurate estimate, round the divisor and the dividend in the same direction, both up OR both down.

Example 21

Estimate the quotient by rounding $5{,}679 \div 37$

$$
\begin{array}{r}
150 \\
40\overline{)6000} \\
-40 \\
\hline
200 \\
-200 \\
\hline
00 \\
\underline{00}
\end{array}
$$

The Average

To find the average: **Add up the numbers, then divide by the number of items you have added.**

Example 22

Find the average of 3, 6, 10, 11, and 15.

$$\frac{3+6+10+11+15}{5} = \frac{45}{5} = 7$$

To find the average of 5 numbers, divide by 5.

-8-

Example 23

A student received the following exam scores: 72, 78, 93. What was the student's average for the three exams?

$$\frac{72 + 78 + 93}{3} = \frac{243}{3} = 81$$

Factoring and Prime Numbers

A prime number is a number that can only be factored by itself and 1. For example, 7 is a prime number because no other number divides into 7 without a remainder except 7 and 1. However, 10 is not a prime number. 10 can be divided by 2 and 5 in addition to 1 and 10. Numbers that are not prime numbers are called *composite* numbers.

To factor a number into primes: **Try to divide it by each prime number successively until you arrive at a prime or pass the square root of the number being factored.**

Example 24

Factor 12 into primes.

$$2\overline{)12}$$
$$2\overline{)\ 6}$$
$$3$$

Try 2.
You are left with 6. Try 2 again.

You are left with 3. 3 is a prime, so you are finished.

12 = 2 x 2 x 3

Example 25

Factor 75 into primes.

$$3\overline{)75}$$
$$5\overline{)25}$$
$$5$$

2 does not work. Try 3.
You are left with 25. Try 5.

You are left with 5, a prime.

75 = 3 x 5 x 5

Divisibility Tests

These are quick ways to check if a number can be divided without a remainder before doing the actual division.

To see if 2 is a factor: **A number can be divided by 2 without a remainder if the number ends in 2, 4, 6, 8, or 0.**

Example 26

a) Is 2 a factor of 45,778?

45,778 can be divided by 2 because it ends in an even number.

b) Is 2 a factor of 682,405?

682,405 cannot be divided by 2 without a remainder because it does not end in 2, 4, 6, 8, or 0.

To see if 3 is a factor: **A number can be divided by 3 without a remainder if the sum of its digits can be divided by 3 without a remainder.**

Example 27

a) Is 3 a factor of 75,439?

7+5+4+3+9=28   Since 28÷3 has a remainder, 3 is not a factor of 75,439.

b) Is 3 a factor of 444?

4+4+4=12   Since 12÷3 has no remainder, 3 is a factor of 444.

To see if 4 is a factor: **A number can be divided by 4 without a remainder if the two-digit number at the end can be evenly divided by 4.**

Example 28

a) Is 4 a factor of 52,814?

14 is not evenly divisible by 4, so neither is 52,814.

b) Is 4 a factor of 357,036?

36 can be evenly divided by 4, so 357,036 is also divisible by 4.

To see if 5 is a factor: **A number can be divided by 5 without a remainder if the last digit is 5 or 0.**

<u>Example 29</u>

a) Is 5 a factor of 560?
   This ends in 0 or 5, so 5 will divide it evenly.

b) Is 5 a factor of 5,006?
   No. 5 will not divide it without a remainder because this number does not end in 5 or 0.

To see if 6 is a factor: **A number can be evenly divided by 6 if the tests for 2 and 3 both work.**

<u>Example 30</u>

a) Is 6 a factor of 2,538?
   2 divides into this number because it ends in an even digit.
   3 divides into this number because the sum of its digits is 18, and 3 divides evenly into 18.
   Therefore, 6 will divide into 2,538.

b) Is 6 a factor of 30,213?
   Although 3 divides evenly into this number, 2 does not, so 6 will not.

To see if 7 is a factor: **There is no simple divisibility test for 7.**

To see if 8 is a factor: **If the number formed by the last three digits is divisible by 8, 8 is a factor.**

<u>Example 31</u>

Is 8 a factor of 245,673,800?
   Since 8 is a factor of 800, 8 divides into the entire number evenly.

To see if 9 is a factor: **A number can be evenly divided by 9 if 9 divides into the sum of the digits.**

<u>Example 32</u>

a) Is 9 a factor of 581?

   5+8+1=14

   Since 9 does not divide evenly into 14, it does not divide evenly into 581.

b) Is 9 a factor of 7,641?

   7+6+4+1=18

   Since 9 divides evenly into 18, it is a factor of 7, 641.

To see if 10 is a factor: **10 divides evenly into numbers ending in 0.**

<u>Example 33</u>

Is 10 a factor of 470?

   470 ends in 0, so 10 will divide it evenly.

Exercises

1. Express the following numbers in words.

   (a) 2,402,363   (b) 5,007
   (c) 255,025,025   (d) 402,300
   (e) 23,000,005   (f) 120,016
   (g) 807,253,510   (h) 10,010
   (i) 11,110,100   (j) 9,090

2. Write the following numbers using numerals.

   (a) three hundred eight thousand, eight.
   (b) fifteen thousand, two hundred
   (c) five million, two
   (d) fourteen thousand, twenty eight
   (e) sixty three million, four hundred twenty nine
   (f) two hundred eight million, five hundred one thousand
   (g) nine thousand, ten
   (h) fifty three thousand, one hundred eleven
   (i) fourteen million, seven hundred thousand
   (j) three hundred three thousand

3. Round the following numbers to the indicated place.

   (a) 57,235,908   (nearest million)
   (b) 13,528,027   (nearest thousand)
   (c) 49,865,200   (nearest hundred thousand)
   (d) 5,397   (nearest ten)
   (e) 48,253   (nearest hundred)
   (f) 10,901   (nearest thousand)
   (g) 604,395   (nearest thousand)
   (h) 196,238   (nearest ten thousand)
   (i) 490,258   (nearest hundred thousand)
   (j) 16,305,299   (nearest hundred thousand)
   (k) 5,999,990   (nearest ten thousand)
   (l) 2,987   (nearest hundred)
   (m) 153,908   (nearest hundred thousand)
   (n) 18,536,253   (nearest million)

4. Estimate each sum. Then check to see how close you are by adding the following numbers.
   (a) 124 + 18 + 937
   (b) 23,000 + 1, 400 + 8,500
   (c) 2,030 + 9,080
   (d) 5,000,733 + 11,006,000 + 45,000

5. Betty earns $125 more each week than Larry earns. If Larry earns $450, how much do Betty and Larry earn together?

6. Estimate each difference. Then check to see how close you are by subtracting the following numbers.
   (a) 50,000 - 12,987
   (b) 40,000 - 12,905
   (c) Subtract 158 from 412
   (d) Subtract 34,234 from 1,000,000
   (e) 439 less than 900

7. Lee had $750 in a checking account. That month Lee deposited 4 paychecks for $497 each. Lee wrote the following checks: $398 rent, $43 telephone bill, $23 electric bill, $98 credit card payment. Lee also withdrew $75 cash from the account 6 times. What was the balance of the account at the end of the month?

8. Estimate each product. Then check to see how close you are by multiplying the following numbers.

   (a) 97 x 68
   (c) 1500 x 120
   (e) 2,000,000 x 9,000

   (b) 203 x 96
   (d) 73,000 x 8,000
   (f) 45 x 98 x 253 x 0

9. If one box of oranges will make 20 four-ounce servings of fresh orange juice, how many boxes will a restaurant need to have on hand for 300 servings?

10. Estimate each quotient. Then check to see how close you are by dividing the following numbers.

   (a) 4,284 divided by 42   (b) 118,118 divided by 59

   (c) $\dfrac{37,500}{500}$ (d) $\dfrac{66,143}{11}$

   (e) 90,693 ÷ 3   (f) 960,400 ÷ 9,800

   (g) 14,000 ÷ 100   (h) 152,000,000 ÷ 10,000

11. A section of fencing is 6 feet long. How many sections will be needed to fence in a rectangular piece of property 50 ft x 100 ft? (Leave out 5 ft for the gate.)

12. A child watched 3 hours of television Monday, 1 hour Tuesday, 0 hours Wednesday, 1 hour Thursday, 3 hours Friday, 5 hours Saturday and 1 hour Sunday. What is the average amount of time this child spends watching TV each day?

13. Factor the numbers below into primes:

   (a) 72   (b) 55   (c) 56
   (d) 36   (e) 121   (f) 200
   (g) 18   (h) 29   (i) 143

14. Use the divisibility test for 2 to determine which of the following numbers has a factor of 2.

(a) 9,010   (b) 2,121   (c) 15,072   (d) 3,338

(e) 24,689   (f) 1,497   (g) 3,333,336   (h) 2,461

15. Use the divisibility test for 3 to determine which of the following numbers has a factor of 3.

(a) 3,173   (b) 281   (c) 12,510   (d) 106,401

(e) 444   (f) 90,840   (g) 113,333   (h) 300,000

16. Use the divisibility test for 4 to determine which of the following numbers has a factor of 4.

(a) 3,316   (b) 15,920   (c) 5,034   (d) 3,400,000

(e) 8,246   (f) 79,264   (g) 114   (h) 314

17. Use the divisibility test for 2 and 3 to determine which of the following numbers has a factor of 6.

(a) 2,460   (b) 105   (c) 3,004   (d) 2,142

(e) 102,600   (f) 6,026   (g) 18,000   (h) 104,220

18. Use the divisibility test for 9 to determine which of the following numbers has a factor of 9.

(a) 34,578   (b) 333   (c) 919   (d) 1,027

(e) 567   (f) 10,999   (g) 67,427   (h) 45,000

Answers

1. (a) two million, four hundred two thousand, three hundred sixty three;
    (b) five thousand, seven;
    (c) two hundred fifty five million, twenty five thousand, twenty five;
    (d) four hundred two thousand, three hundred;
    (e) twenty three million, five;   (f) one hundred twenty thousand, sixteen;
    (g) eight hundred seven million, two hundred fifty three thousand, five hundred ten;
    (h) ten thousand, ten;
    (i) eleven million, one hundred ten thousand, one hundred;
    (j) nine thousand, ninety

2. (a) 308,008;   (b) 15,200;   (c) 49,900,000;   (d) 14,028;
    (e) 63,000,429;   (f) 208,501,000; (g) 9,010;   (h) 53,111;
    (i) 14,700,000;   (j) 303,000

3. (a) 57,000,000;   (b) 13,528,000; (c) 49,00,000;   (d) 5,400;
    (e) 48,300;   (f) 11,000;   (g) 604,000;   (h) 200,000;
    (i) 500,000;   (j) 16,300,000; (k) 6,000,000;   (l) 3,000;
    (m) 200,000;   (n) 19,000,000

4. (a) 1,079;   (b) 32,900;   (c) 11,110;   (d) 16,051,733

5. $1,025

6. (a) 37,013;   (b) 27,095;   (c) 254;   (d) 965,766;
    (e) 461

7. $1,726

8. (a) 6,596;   (b) 19,488;   (c) 180,000;   (d) 584,000,000;
    (e) 18,000,000,000; (f) 0

9. 15

10. (a) 102;   (b) 2,002;   (c) 75;   (d) 6,013;
    (e) 30,231;   (f) 98;   (g) 140;   (h) 15,200

11. 50 sections   12. 2 hours

13.   (a) 2 x 2 x 2 x 3 x 3;   (b) 5 x 11;   (c) 2 x 2 x 2 x 7;
       (d) 2 x 2 x 3 x 3;   (e) 11 x 11;
       (f) 2 x 2 x 2 x 5 x 5;   (g) 2 x 3 x 3;   (h) 29 is prime
      (i) 11 x 13

14. (a) 9,010;   (c) 15,072;   (d) 3,338;   (g) 3,333,336

15. (c) 12,510; (d) 106,401;   (e) 444;   (f) 90,840;   (h) 300,000

16. (a) 3,316;   (b) 15,920;   (d) 3,400,000;   (f) 79,264

17. (a) 2,460;   (d) 2,142;   (e) 102,600;   (g) 18,000;   (h) 104,220

18. (a) 34,578;   (b) 333;   (e) 567;   (h) 45,000

MEASUREMENT

Units of measure and equivalents

Measures of Length
1 foot (ft.)	= 12 inches (in.)
1 yard (yd.)	= 3 feet (ft.)
1 mile (mi.)	= 1,760 yards = 5,280 feet

Measures of Weight
1 pound (lb.)	= 16 ounces (oz.)
1 ton	= 2,000 pounds

Measures of Volume
1 pint (pt.)	= 16 fluid ounces (fl. oz.)
1 quart (qt.)	= 2 pints
1 gallon (gal.)	= 4 quarts

Measures of Time
1 minute (min.)	= 60 seconds (sec.)
1 hour (hr.)	= 60 minutes
1 day (da.)	= 24 hours
1 week (wk.)	= 7 days
1 month (mo.)	= 4 weeks (approx.)
1 year (yr.)	= 12 months

Measures of Counting
1 dozen (doz.)	= 12 units
1 gross (gr.)	= 12 dozen = 144 units

Addition of units of measurement

To add units of measurement:
1. Add the corresponding units
2. Simplify the solution by:
    a. converting smaller unit into larger unit (when possible), and
    b. adding onto larger unit.

Example 1

```
    1 gallon    2 quarts          Add the corresponding units.
  + 5 gallons   1 quart
    6 gallons   3 quarts
```

Example 2

```
    2 feet    7 inches
  + 5 feet    8 inches
    7 feet    15 inches          Replace 15 inches with 1 foot 3 inches and
  + 1 foot    3 inches           add.
    8 feet    3 inches
```

Subtraction of units of measurement

To subtract units of measurement:
1. Subtract the corresponding units.
2. If necessary, borrow 1 unit from the larger unit, convert to smaller unit, and add onto smaller unit. Then proceed with step 1.

Example 3

```
    12 pounds   11 ounces
  -  4 pounds    8 ounces          Subtract the corresponding units.
     8 pounds    3 ounces
```

Example 4

<table>
<tr><td></td><td>5 hours</td><td>35 minutes</td></tr>
<tr><td></td><td>- 2 hours</td><td>52 minutes</td></tr>
</table>

<table>
<tr><td>4</td><td></td><td>95</td><td></td></tr>
<tr><td>5̶ hours</td><td></td><td>3̶5̶ minutes</td><td></td></tr>
<tr><td>- 2 hours</td><td></td><td>52 minutes</td><td></td></tr>
<tr><td>2 hours</td><td></td><td>43 minutes</td><td></td></tr>
</table>

It is necessary to convert 1 hour, which you borrow from the 5 hours, into 60 minutes.

Add the 60 minutes onto the 35 minutes you already have.

35 minutes
+ 60 minutes
95 minutes

Exercises

1. Addition of units of measurement

(a)   3 feet   2 inches
  + 5 feet   8 inches

(b)   5 hours   42 minutes
  + 3 hours   17 minutes

(c)   4 pounds   12 ounces
  + 3 pounds   6 ounces

(d)   3 miles   1000 yards
  + 2 miles   1000 yards

(e)   3 gallons   3 quarts
  + 4 gallons   1 quart

(f)   3 gross   4 dozen
  + 7 gross   9 dozen

2. Subtraction of units of measurement

(a)   5 hours   20 minutes
  - 3 hours   15 minutes

(b)   5 years   7 months
  - 2 years   4 months

(c)   4 gallons   2 quarts
  - 1 gallon   3 quarts

(d)   12 days   15 hours
  - 8 days   20 hours

(e)   2 quarts   1 pint
  - 1 quart

(f)   10 yards   7 inches
  - 6 yards   9 inches

3. Applications

(a) A 3 yard 1 foot shelf was cut to 1 yard 2 feet. How big a piece was cut off the shelf?

(b) Marc studied 3 hours 45 minutes for his math exam on Tuesday, and an additional 5 hours 35 minutes for his science exam. How much did he study altogether?

(c) After a strenuous aerobics workout, Maxine found that she weighed 112 pounds 8 ounces. This indicated a loss of 1 pound 10 ounces due to the workout. How much did she weigh before the aerobics workout?

(d) Out of a delivery of $7\frac{1}{2}$ dozen eggs, 18 eggs were found to be broken. How many dozen eggs remained?

(e) A marathon runner ran 26 miles in the New York City Marathon. This was 15 miles 300 yards more than she usually runs on her high school track. What distance does she normally run?

(f) Jimmy has been taking piano lessons for 3 years 7 months. Before a scheduled piano recital, he will have an additional 7 months of lessons. At the time of the recital, how long will he have been taking lessons?

Answers

1. (a) 8 feet 10 inches;   (b) 8 hours 59 minutes;   (c) 8 pounds 2 ounces;
    (d) 6 miles 240 yards   (e) 8 gallons;   (f) 11 gross 1 dozen;

2. (a) 2 hours 5 minutes; (b) 3 years 3 months;   (c) 2 gallons 3 quarts;
    (d) 3 days 19 hours;   (e) 1 quart 1 pint;   (f) 3 yards 34 inches

3. (a) 1 yard 2 feet;   (b) 9 hours 20 minutes;   (c) 114 pounds 2 ounces;
    (d) 6 dozen;   (e) 10 miles 1460 yards;   (f) 4 years 2 months

DECIMAL NUMBERS

Converting Decimal Numbers

To change a decimal number to a fraction or a mixed number:

1. All digits to the left of the decimal point become the whole number part of the mixed number. If there is a zero or no digit to the left of the decimal point, the decimal number converts to a proper fraction.
2. The digits to the right of the decimal point become the numerator of the fraction.
3. Place a 1 in the denominator, followed be a zero for each digit to the right of the decimal point.
4. Simplify the resulting fraction if possible.

Example 1

Change 0.637 to a fraction

$$\frac{637}{1000}$$

Three digits after the decimal point require three zeros in the denominator.

Example 2

Change 53.02 to a fraction.

$$53\frac{02}{100} = 53\frac{1}{50}$$

Expressing a Decimal Number in Words

To express a decimal number in words: **A decimal number is expressed in words the same way that a fractional number is expressed in words.**

Example 3

Translate 405.239 into words.

$$405\frac{239}{1000}$$

Four hundred five and two hundred thirty nine thousandths.

Rounding Decimal Numbers

To round a decimal number to a specified place:

1. Locate the place you will round to. (The tenths place is one digit to the right of the decimal point. The hundredths place is two digits to the right of the decimal point. The thousandths place is three digits to the right of the decimal point.
2. Drop all of the digits to the right of the place you will round to.
3. If the first digit dropped was 5 or greater, add 1 to the last digit of your new shortened number. Otherwise, stop.

Example 4

Round to the nearest hundredth

    1359.2468

    Drop all digits after the 4. Since 6 was the first digit dropped and it is 5 or greater, add 1 to the 4.

    1359.25

Example 5

Round to the nearest tenth

    0.7429

    Drop all digits after the 7. Since 4 was the first digit dropped and it is not 5 or greater, stop.

    0.7

Example 6

Round to the nearest hundredth

    475.9987

    476.00

Comparing Decimal Numbers

To compare decimal numbers
1. Count the number of digits to the right of the decimal point in the number with the most digits to the right of the decimal point.
2. Attach zeros to the ends of the other numbers being compared so all numbers have an equal number of digits to the right of the decimal point. (This does not change the values of the decimal numbers. It is similar to building equivalent fractions in order to have common denominators.)
3. Compare the numbers.

Example 7

Write the following decimal numbers in order from smallest to largest

.203, .32, .3, .033

Rewrite:

.203, .320, .300, .033

In order:

.033, .203, .300, .320

Or:

.033, .203, .3, .32

Note: All zeros after the last non-zero digit to the right of the decimal point can be deleted. this does not change the value of the number. It is similar to simplifying a fraction.

Adding and Subtracting Decimal Numbers

To add decimal numbers: **Line up the decimal points vertically. If a number has no decimal point, it is a whole number and the decimal point is attached on the far right. Bring the decimal point straight down for the answer.**

Example 8

Add 23.8, 34 and 107.65

```
  23.8
  34.
 107.65
 165.45
```

To subtract decimal numbers: Line up the decimal points. Attach zeros after the decimal point to fill all empty places. Then subtract. Bring the decimal point straight down for the answer.

Example 9

15.9 - 8.76

```
    15.90
  - 8.76
    7.14
```

Example 10

Subtract 8.95 from 15.

```
    15.00
  - 8.95
    6.05
```

Place a decimal point at the end of the whole number 15, followed by zeros.

To estimate adding and subtracting decimal numbers: **Round to the nearest whole number. If the number is less than 1, round to the nearest tenth. Then add or subtract.**

Multiplying Decimal Numbers

To multiply decimal numbers

1. Line up the numbers all the way to the right as if there were no decimal points. Multiply as you would whole numbers.
2. To determine the location of the decimal point in the product, add the number of digits to the right of the decimal point in both numbers being multiplied. This total is the number of digits that will be to the right of the decimal point in the answer.
3. Starting to the right of the product, count back and place the decimal point. If there are not enough digits, add zeros on the left and keep counting back.

<u>Example 11</u>

$$
\begin{array}{r}
.231 \\
\underline{\times\ .18} \\
1848 \\
\underline{231\ \ } \\
4158
\end{array}
$$

= .04158

Note: Line up the digits, not the decimal points when you multiply.

The total number of decimal places is 5, so one zero needs to be added on the left.

To multiply a decimal number by a power of 10: **Move the decimal point to the right one space for each zero in the power of 10.**

<u>Example 12</u>

.045 x 100

4.5

Move the decimal point 2 spaces to the right because 100 is 10^2 (or has 2 zeros).

Converting a Fraction to a Decimal Number

To convert a fraction to a decimal number: **Divide the numerator by the denominator.**
1. The numerator becomes the dividend. Place a decimal point at the end of the dividend.
2. Bring the decimal point straight up for the quotient.
3. Attach a zero after the decimal point in the dividend. Divide. Attach zeros to the dividend until there is no remainder or there are enough digits in the quotient to round to a specified place.

<u>Example 13</u>

Express $\frac{4}{5}$ as a decimal.

$$
\begin{array}{r}
0.8\ \ \\
5{\overline{\smash{)}\,4.0}} \\
\underline{4\ 0\ } \\
0
\end{array}
$$

= 0.8

Example 14

Express $\frac{1}{11}$ as a decimal number rounded to the nearest hundredth.

$$\begin{array}{r} 0.090 \\ 11\overline{)1.000} \\ \underline{99} \\ 10 \end{array}$$

≈ 0.09

This will give enough digits to round back one place to the nearest hundredth.
There is no need to continue dividing.
Round.

Example 15

Change $4\frac{2}{3}$ to a decimal number and round to the nearest tenth.

$$\begin{array}{r} .66 \\ 3\overline{)2.00} \\ \underline{1\,8} \\ 20 \\ \underline{18} \\ 2 \end{array}$$

≈ 4.7

This work is for the decimal part of the number. The whole number 4 will be to the left of the decimal point.

Round the quotient .66...

Division of Decimal numbers

To divide a decimal number by a whole number: **Bring the decimal point straight up for the quotient. Attach zeros to the dividend until either there is no remainder or there are enough digits to round to a specified place.**

Example 16

$3.8 \div 12$ and round the answer to the nearest hundredth.

$$\begin{array}{r} 0.316 \\ 12\overline{)3.800} \\ \underline{3\,6} \\ 20 \\ \underline{12} \\ 80 \\ \underline{72} \end{array}$$

≈ 0.32

To divide by a decimal number

1. If there is no decimal point in the dividend, put one on the far right (at the end).
2. Make the divisor look like a whole number by sliding the decimal point all the way to the right. Count how many places the decimal point was moved.
3. Move the decimal point in the dividend the same number of places that you moved the decimal point in the divisor.
4. Follow the procedure for dividing a decimal number by a whole number.

Example 17

$1.3 \div .53$ Round the answer to the nearest hundredth.

```
        .53.)1.30.
         ➔➔  ➔➔

             002.452
        53)130.000
           106
            24 0
            21 2
             2 80
             2 65
               150
               106
        ≈ 2.45
```

This gives enough digits to round back to the hundredths

Example 18

$12 \div .4$

```
            .4.)12.0.
             ➔    ➔

                30
            4)120


          = 30
```

Note: Remember to put the decimal point at the end of the whole number dividend.

To divide a decimal number by a power of 10: **Move the decimal point one place to the left for each zero in the power of 10.**

<u>Example 19</u>

   $5.683 \div 1000$

   .005.683
   ←←←

   = .005683

There are 3 zeros in 1000 or 10^3, so move the decimal point 3 places to the left in 5.683

Exercises

1. Change the following decimal numbers to fractions. Reduce to lowest terms if possible.

(a)	5.99	(b)	45.21	(c)	0.7
(d)	0.987	(e)	0.71	(f)	.007
(g)	908.607	(h)	100.03	(i)	32.8
(j)	65.2	(k)	1.24	(l)	3.78
(m)	15.15	(n)	0.75	(o)	890.08
(p)	100.005	(q)	34.506	(r)	.37

2. Express the following decimal numbers in words.

(a)	204.54	(b)	7568.06	(c)	3.659
(d)	0.905	(e)	40.6	(f)	900.007
(g)	7.01	(h)	345,607.304	(i)	10,005.43
(j)	120,020.0003				

3. Express the following as decimal numbers.
   (a) fourteen and fifteen hundredths
   (b) eight and two hundred twenty thousandths
   (c) five hundred and four tenths
   (d) thirty-one and nine hundredths
   (e) nineteen and one thousandth
   (f) eighty and seven tenths
   (g) forty-four and fifty-three hundredths
   (h) two tenths
   (i) ten and three tenths
   (j) one hundred four and nine tenths
   (k) three thousand and four thousandths
   (l) one and twenty five ten thousandths
   (m) sixteen thousand two and eleven hundredths
   (n) eighty-one hundred thousandths

4. Round the following numbers to the nearest tenth.

    (a) 56.125   (b) 8.8999   (c) 211.1115

    (d) 17.898   (e) 340.09732   (f) 2.9192

    (g) 89,785.8809   (h) 0.907   (i) 0.9973

5. Round the following numbers to the nearest hundredth.

    (a) 203.342   (b) 0.7409   (c) 98.0003

    (d) 4.5678   (e) 23.76543   (f) 95.15099

    (g) 0.9999   (h) 999.999   (i) 800.894

6. Rewrite each group in order from smallest to largest.

    (a) 5.54, 5.055, 5.6, .599, 5.5

    (b) .123, .13, .21, .2, .032

    (c) 0.87, 0.9, 0.088, 0.09, 0.7

    (d) 35.6, 35.08, 3.999, 3.56, 35.068

    (e) 12.3, 12.03, 12.333, 12.003, 12.25

    (f) .36, .037, .3, .007, .073

7. Add

    (a) .23+.67   (b) 2.5+8.9

    (c) .2+.98+.6   (d) 34.6+48.97

    (e) 3+4.5   (f) 123.8+451

    (g) 8+123.5+.62   (h) .28+125.92

    (i) 1+.2+.03   (j) 451.32+1027.58+43.004

    (k) 1.5+.26+37   (l) .3+3+5.01

8. Subtract

    (a) .78 - .56   (b) 9.3 - 4.8

    (c) 18.3 - 5.67   (d) 803.9 - 156.76

    (e) 20 - 1.27   (f) 12.53 - 8

    (g) 15.5 - .25   (h) 13 - .99

    (i) 123.75 - .893   (j) 3 - .007

9. Multiply

(a) 2.3 x .23   (b) 7 x .08   (c) .1 x .03

(d) .93 x .76   (e) .82 x 7.5   (f) 128.35 x .04

(g) .027 x 6   (h) 101 x .01   (i) 300 x .009

10. Multiply

(a) 10 x .03   (b) 100 x .08   (c) 1000 x .05

(d) 7.2 x 10   (e) 8.3 x 100   (f) 9.5 x 1000

(g) .006 x 10   (h) .006 x 100   (i) .006 x 1000

11. Convert the fractions or mixed numbers to decimal numbers. If they do not terminate, round the answer to the nearest hundredth.

(a) $\frac{3}{10}$ (b) $\frac{5}{8}$ (c) $\frac{7}{9}$

(d) $\frac{5}{11}$ (e) $\frac{2}{3}$ (f) $\frac{6}{7}$

(g) $5\frac{3}{8}$ (h) $10\frac{1}{5}$ (i) $1\frac{3}{4}$

(j) $21\frac{3}{14}$ (k) $18\frac{2}{9}$ (l) $124\frac{7}{8}$

(m) $3\frac{5}{6}$ (n) $44\frac{1}{11}$ (o) $20\frac{19}{20}$

12. Divide. If the quotient does not terminate, round it to the nearest hundredth.

(a) $7\overline{)4.921}$ (b) $101\overline{)9.2}$ (c) $9\overline{).0918}$

(d) 12.3 ÷ 5   (e) .17 ÷ 3   (f) .205 ÷ 18

(g) 12.8 ÷ 19   (h) 72.3 ÷ 7   (i) .059 ÷ 50

(j) 800.3 ÷ 9   (k) 20.207 ÷ 25   (l) 4.238 ÷ 30

(m) 0.2 ÷ 500   (n) 0.75 ÷ 25   (o) 0.9 ÷ 27

13. Divide. If the quotient does not terminate, round it to the nearest hundredth.

    (a) $.3\overline{)2.1}$ (b) $.5\overline{)1.805}$ (c) $.01\overline{)5.12}$

    (d) $6 \div .03$ (e) $10 \div .25$ (f) $.38 \div .02$

    (g) $.037 \div .18$ (h) $710 \div .54$ (i) $2 \div .009$

    (j) Divide 18 by .09   (k) Divide 3.5 by .007

    (l) Divide .09 by .27   (m) Divide 7 by .07

    (n) Divide 63 by .009   (o) Divide 1000 by .1

    (p) Divide 15 by .15   (q) Divide 8.5 by 5.5

14. Divide

    (a) $.03 \div 10$ (b) $.08 \div 100$ (c) $.05 \div 1000$

    (d) $7.2 \div 100$ (e) $9.5 \div 1000$ (f) $83 \div 100$

15. A student purchased a pen for $1.98, a notebook for $4.40 and a textbook for $32.95. How much change should the student receive from a $50 bill?

16. Find length a

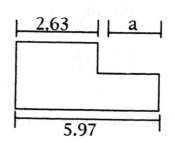

17. Find length b

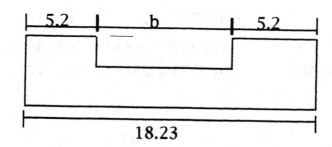

-34-

18. Find length c.

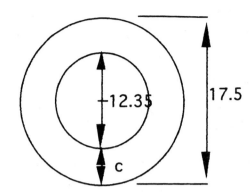

19. A technical assistant earns $418.75 an hour. If the assistant receives a raise of $1.50 an hour, how much more will the assistant receive for a 35-hour week?

20. If a stock is selling for $42.75 a share, how many shares will an investor receive for $4617?

Answers

1. (a) $5\frac{99}{100}$;   (b) $45\frac{21}{100}$;   (c) $\frac{7}{10}$;   (d) $\frac{987}{1000}$;

   (e) $\frac{71}{100}$;   (f) $\frac{7}{1000}$;   (g) $908\frac{607}{1000}$;   (h) $100\frac{3}{100}$;

   (i) $32\frac{4}{5}$;   (j) $65\frac{1}{5}$;   (k) $1\frac{6}{25}$;   (l) $3\frac{39}{50}$;

   (m) $15\frac{3}{20}$;   (n) $\frac{3}{4}$;   (o) $890\frac{2}{25}$;   (p) $100\frac{1}{200}$;

   (q) $34\frac{253}{500}$;   (r) $\frac{37}{100}$

2. (a) two hundred four and fifty-four hundredths;
   (b) seven thousand, five hundred sixty eight and six hundredths;
   (c) three and six hundred fifty-nine thousandths;
   (d) nine hundred five thousandths;
   (e) forty and six tenths;
   (f) nine hundred and seven thousandths;
   (g) seven and one hundredth;
   (h) three hundred forty five thousand, six hundred seven and three hundred four thousandths;
   (i) ten thousand, five and forty three hundredths;
   (j) one hundred twenty thousand, twenty and three ten thousandths

3. (a) 14.15;   (b) 8.220;   (c) 500.4;   (d) 31.09;   (e) 19.001;
   (f) 80.7;   (g) 44.53;   (h) .2;   (i) 10.3;   (j) 104.9;
      (k) 3000.004;   (l) 1.0025;   (m) 16,002.11;   (n) .00081

4. (a) 56.1;   (b) 8.9;   (c) 211.1;   (d) 17.9;   (e) 340.1;
   (f) 2.9;   (g) 89,785.9;   (h) 0.9;   (i) 1.0

5. (a) 203.34;   (b) 0.74;   (c) 98.00   (d) 4.57;   (e) 23.77;
   (f) 95.15;   (g) 1.00;   (h) 1000.00;   (i) 800.89

6. (a) .599, 5.055, 5.5, 5.54, 5.6;
   (b) .032, .123, .13, .2, .21;
   (c) 0.088, 0.09, 0.7, 0.87, 0.9;   (d) 3.56, 3.999, 35.068, 35.08, 35.6;
   (e) 12.003, 12.03, 12.25, 12.3, 12.333;
   (f) .007, .037, .073, .3, .36

7. (a) .9;   (b) 11.4;   (c) 1.78;   (d) 83.57;   (e) 7.5;
   (f) 574.8;   (g) 132.12;   (h) 126.2;   (i) 1.23;   (j) 1521.904;
   (k) 38.76;   (l) 8.31

8. (a) .22;   (b) 4.5;   (c) 12.63;   (d) 647.14;   (e) 18.73;
   (f) 4.53;   (g) 15.25;   (h) 12.01;   (i) 122.857;   (j) 2.993

9. (a) .529;   (b) .56;   (c) .003;   (d) .7068;   (e) 6.15;
   (f) 5.134;   (g) .162;   (h) 1.01;   (i) 2.7

10. (a) .3;   (b) 8;   (c) 50;   (d) 72;   (e) 830;
    (f) 9500;   (g) .06;   (h) .6;   (i) 6

11. (a) .3;   (b) .625;   (c) .78;   (d) .45;   (e) .67;
    (f) .86;   (g) 5.375;   (h) 10.2;   (i) 1.75;   (j) 21.21;
    (k) 18.22;   (l) 124.875;   (m) 3.83;   (n) 44.09;   (o) 20.95

12. (a) .703;   (b) .09;   (c) .0102;   (d) 2.46;   (e) .06;
    (f) .01;   (g) .67;   (h) 10.33;   (i) .00118;   (j) 88.92;
    (k) 0.80828;   (l) 0.14;   (m) 0.0004;   (n) 0.03;   (o) 0.03

13. (a) 7;   (b) 3.61;   (c) 512;   (d) 200;   (e) 40;
    (f) 19;   (g) 0.21;   (h) 1314.81;   (i) 222.22;   (j) 200;
    (k) 500;   (l) .33;   (m) 100;   (n) 7000;   (o) 10000;
    (p) 100;   (q) 1.55

14. (a) .003;   (b) .0008;   (c) .00005;   (d) .072;   (e) .0095;
    (f) .83

15. $10.67;

16. 3.34;

17. 7.83;

18. 2.575;

19. $52.50;

20. 108

PERCENTS

Before we can discuss percents we must first understand ratios.

Ratio

A ratio is a comparison between two numbers or quantities.

A ratio of 2 to 3 can be written as 2:3 or $\frac{2}{3}$.

The meaning of percent

A percent is a ratio in which a number is compared to 100.

8% is the same as $\frac{8}{100}$.

Converting percents to fraction and decimal numbers

To change a percent to a fraction or decimal number:
1. Drop the % sign.
2. Divide by 100.

Example 1

Change 17% to a fraction in simplest form.

$$17\% = 17 \div 100 \text{ or } \frac{17}{100}$$

Example 2

Change $8\frac{1}{2}\%$ to a fraction in simplest form.

$$8\frac{1}{2}\% = 8\frac{1}{2} \div 100$$

$$= \frac{17}{2} \div \frac{100}{1}$$

$$= \frac{17}{2} \times \frac{1}{100}$$

$$= \frac{17}{200}$$

Change to improper fractions.
Change ÷ to x .
Invert the second fraction.

Example 3

Change 4.7% to a decimal number.

$$4.7\% = 4.7 \div 100$$

$$= .047$$

When you divide by 100 you move the decimal point two places to the left.

04.7 ÷ 100

Add a zero to hold the place

Example 4

Change 26% to a decimal number.

$$26\% = 26 \div 100$$
$$= 26. \div 100$$

$$= .26$$

Any whole number can have a decimal point placed to its right.

26 = 26.
Move the decimal point two places to the left when dividing by 100.

26.

Example 5

Change $12\frac{3}{4}\%$ to a decimal number.

$$12\frac{3}{4}\% = 12.75\%$$
$$= 12.75 \div 100$$

To change a fraction into a decimal number, divide the denominator into the numerator

$$\begin{array}{r} .75 \\ 4\overline{)3.00} \\ \underline{28} \\ 20 \\ \underline{20} \end{array}$$

To change the % to a decimal number, divide by 100. Move the decimal point two places to the left to divide by 100.
12.75

$$= .1275$$

Converting fractions and decimal numbers into percents

To change a fraction or decimal number into a percent:
1. **Multiply by 100**
2. **Attach a % sign.**

Example 6

Change 14.5 into a percent.

$$14.5 \times 100 = 1450.$$

Multiply by 100 and attach a % sign. When you multiply by 100, you move the decimal point two places to the right.

14.50.

Add a zero to hold the place.

The decimal point to the right of a whole number is understood and does not have to be written.

$$= 1450\%$$

Example 7

Change $\frac{3}{8}$ to a percent.

$$\overset{25}{\underset{2}{\frac{3}{\cancel{8}}}} \times \frac{\cancel{100}}{1} = \frac{75}{2}\%$$

Multiply by 100 and attach a % sign. Remember to cancel by dividing numerator and denominator by 4.

Simplify your answer by changing it to a mixed number.

$$= 37\frac{1}{2}\%$$

Alternate Method:

$$\frac{3}{8} = .375$$

$$.375 \times 100 = 37.5\%$$

Dividing 8 into 3 gives .375

When you multiply by 100, move the decimal point two places to the right.
.37.5

<u>Example 8</u>

Change $.004\frac{1}{2}$ into a percent.

$.004\frac{1}{2} = .0045$

Dividing 2 into 1 we find that
$\frac{1}{2} = .5$

$.0045 \times 100 = .45\%$

Multiply by 100 and attach a % sign.
When you multiply by 100, you move the
decimal point two places to the right.
.00.45

Finding the percent of a number

To find the percent of a number:
1. Change your percent into a decimal number or fraction
2. Multiply

Note: You may not use a percent when doing
calculations. You must first change your
percent to a fraction or decimal number.

<u>Example 9</u>

Find 12% of 53.

12% could be changed to a fraction or a decimal number.

Method 1 (Change % to a fraction):

$12\% = \frac{12}{100} = \frac{3}{25}$

Change your percent to a fraction and
simplify by dividing the numerator and
denominator by 4.

$\frac{3}{25} \times \frac{53}{1} = \frac{159}{25} = 6\frac{9}{25}$

Multiply by 53 and simplify your answer.

Method 2 (Change % to a decimal number):

$12\% = .12$

Change your percent to a decimal number.

$$\begin{array}{r} 53 \\ \times\ .12 \\ \hline 106 \\ 53 \\ \hline 6.36 \end{array}$$

Multiply.

Note: $6\frac{9}{25} = 6.36$ so either answer is
acceptable.

-40-

Example 10

A dinner for two at your favorite restaurant comes to $37.50. You wish to leave a 20% tip. How much should you leave?

$$20\% = .20$$

$$\begin{array}{r} \$37.50 \\ \times\ .20 \\ \hline \$7.5000 \end{array}$$

Change the % to a decimal number because you are taking a % of a decimal number.

Multiply

You should leave $7.50 for the tip.

An alternate method is the proportion method. This appears on the next page.

Example 11

A druggist needs to use $3\frac{1}{3}\%$ alcohol when mixing a 4 fluid ounce prescription for cough medicine. How much alcohol should he include?

$$3\frac{1}{3}\% = 3\frac{1}{3} \div 100$$

$$= \frac{10}{3} \times \frac{1}{100}$$

$$= \frac{1}{30}$$

$$\frac{1}{30} \times \frac{4}{1} = \frac{4}{30} = \frac{2}{15}$$

Change the percent to a fraction.

Note: $3\frac{1}{3}$ should be changed into a fraction rather than a decimal number since $\frac{1}{3} = .33... = .\overline{3}$, a non-terminating decimal number.

Also see the Proportion Method for Example 11.

Solving percent problems using the proportion method

This method can also be used to find a % of a number.

Proportion: A equation in which two fractions are set equal to each other.

$\frac{1}{2} = \frac{2}{4}$ is a proportion.

If 2 fractions are proportional, when you cross-multiply you will have equality.

$$\frac{1}{2} = \frac{2}{4}$$

$$1 \times 4 = 2 \times 2$$

$$4 = 4$$

If $\frac{a}{b} = \frac{c}{d}$ you can use cross multiplication to solve the problem.

$$a \times d = b \times c$$

Type 1: Finding the "is" (part), "of" (whole), or %.

Since % is based upon comparing a number to 100, a % problem can be solved by using one of the following proportions:

$$\frac{\text{is}}{\text{of}} = \frac{\%}{100} \quad \text{or} \quad \frac{\text{part}}{\text{whole}} = \frac{\%}{100}$$

Note: With this method, you do not have to change your percent into a decimal number or fraction, since the percent is always written as $\frac{\%}{100}$.

Finding the "is" (part)

Examples 9, 10 and 11 can be done using this Proportion Method.

Example 9 (Proportion Method)

Find 12% of 53

$$\frac{\text{is}}{\text{of}} = \frac{\%}{100}$$

$$\frac{n}{53} = \frac{12}{100}$$

$$100n = 636$$

$$\frac{100n}{100} = \frac{636}{100}$$

$$n = 6.36$$

Substitute using: is = n
                                   of = 53
                                   % = 12

Cross-multiply.

To solve, divide by 100.
Remember, when you divide by 100, move your decimal point two places to the left.
6.36.

Example 10 (Proportion Method)

A dinner for two at your favorite restaurant comes to \$37.50. You wish to leave a 20% tip. How much should you leave?

$$\frac{part}{whole} = \frac{\%}{100}$$

Substitute using   part = n
whole = 37.50
% = 20

$$\frac{n}{37.50} = \frac{20}{100}$$

$$\frac{100n}{100} = \frac{750}{100}$$

Cross-multiply and divide by 100.

$$n = \$7.50$$

Example 11 (Proportion Method)

A druggist needs to use $3\frac{1}{3}\%$ alcohol when mixing a 4 fluid ounce prescription for cough medicine. How much alcohol should he include?

$$\frac{part}{whole} = \frac{\%}{100}$$

Substitute using: part = n
whole = 4
$\% = 3\frac{1}{3}$

$$\frac{n}{4} = \frac{3\frac{1}{3}}{100}$$

$$100n = 4 \times 3\frac{1}{3}$$

Cross-multiply

$$= \frac{4}{1} \times \frac{10}{3}$$

$$= \frac{40}{3}$$

$$\frac{100n}{100} = \frac{40}{3} \div \frac{100}{1}$$

Divide by 100

$$n = \frac{40}{3} \times \frac{1}{100}$$

$$= \frac{2}{15} \text{ fluid ounces of alcohol}$$

Finding the "of" (whole)

Example 12

15.5 is 18% of what number? Round the answer to the nearest tenth.

$$\frac{is}{of} = \frac{\%}{100}$$

$$\frac{15.5}{n} = \frac{18}{100}$$

$$\frac{18n}{18} = \frac{1550}{18}$$

Substitute using: is = 15.5
    of = n
    % = 18

Cross-multiply and divide by 18.

Remember: When multiplying by 100, move your decimal point two places to the right.

Add a zero. The decimal point is understood.

15.50. = 1550

$n = 86.1$ (to the nearest tenth)

When rounding to the nearest tenth carry out your division to the hundredths column and round back to the tenths column.
The number in the hundredths column must be 5 or more in order to raise the number in the tenths column by 1.

```
        86.11
   18)1550.00
       144
       110
       108
        20
        18
         2
```

Example 13

A real estate agent earns a commission of 6% on the sale of a house. What should the selling price of the house be so the real estate agent can earn $15,000?

$$\frac{part}{whole} = \frac{\%}{100}$$

$$\frac{15,000}{n} = \frac{6}{100}$$

$$\frac{6n}{n} = \frac{1,500,000}{6}$$

$$n = \$250,000$$

You need to determine:
6% of what is $15,000?

Substitute using   part = 15,000
    whole = n
    % = 6

Cross-multiply and divide by 6.
Remember: When multiplying a whole number by 100, add two zeros.

-44-

The house should sell for $250,000 in order for the agent to earn $15,000.

Finding the %
<u>Example 14</u>

$\frac{3}{8}$ is what percent of 200?

$$\frac{\text{is}}{\text{of}} = \frac{\%}{100}$$

Substitute using $\text{is} = \frac{3}{8}$
$\text{of} = 200$
$\% = n$

$$\frac{\frac{3}{8}}{200} = \frac{n}{100}$$

Cross-multiply

$$200n = \frac{3}{8} \times \frac{100}{1}$$

$$= \frac{75}{2}$$

$$\frac{200n}{200} = \frac{75}{2} \div \frac{200}{1}$$

Divide by 200.

$$= \frac{75}{2} \times \frac{1}{200}$$

$$= \frac{3}{16}$$

Note: You must include the % sign since you are being asked to find a %.

$$n = \frac{3}{16}\%$$

-45-

<u>Example 15</u>

In a town with a population of 10,700 there are 418 doctors. Find to the nearest percent, what percent of the total population of the town is represented by doctors.

$$\frac{part}{whole} = \frac{\%}{100}$$

Substitute using   part = 418
whole = 10,700
% = n

$$\frac{418}{10,700} = \frac{n}{100}$$

$$\frac{10,700n}{10,700} = \frac{41,800}{10,7000}$$

Cross-multiply and divide by 10,700.

$$= \frac{418}{107}$$

Simplify your fraction by dividing the numerator and denominator by 100. This will result in an easier division example.

$$\begin{array}{r} 3.9 \\ 107\overline{)418.0} \quad \approx 4\% \\ \underline{321} \\ 970 \\ \underline{963} \\ 7 \end{array}$$

n = 4% (to the nearest percent)

Approximately 4% of the people of this town are doctors.

Type 2: Solving applications involving discounts, mark-ups, percent of decrease and percent of increase.

Use: $\dfrac{\textbf{change}}{\textbf{original}} = \dfrac{\textbf{\%}}{\textbf{100}}$

Discount (Mark-up) Problems
To find a discounted (or marked-up) price:
1. Find the amount of the discount (or mark-up)
2. a. If a discount problem, subtract the amount of the discount from the original price.
   b. If a mark-up problem, add the amount of the mark-up to the original price.

Note: In the given proportion, the change represents the amount of the discount or mark-up, depending on the problem.

Example 16

A stereo normally selling for $89.00 is advertised as "30% off". What would be the advertised price of the stereo (not including tax)?

You must first determine what is 30% of $89.00.

Method 1:	Method 2: Proportion Method

Method 1:

$30\% = .30$

$$\begin{array}{r} \$89 \\ \times\ .30 \\ \hline \$26.70 \end{array}$$

Method 2: Proportion Method

$$\frac{\text{discount}}{\text{original}} = \frac{\%}{100}$$

Substitute using: discount = n
original = 89
% = 30

$$\frac{n}{89} = \frac{30}{100}$$

$$\frac{100n}{100} = \frac{2670}{100}$$ Cross-multiply and divide by 100.

$$n = \$26.70$$ This represents the amount of the discount.

Subtract the discount from the original price.

$$\begin{array}{r} \$89.00 \\ -26.70 \\ \hline \$62.30 \end{array}$$

The advertised price would be $62.30.

Example 17

Due to increased costs, a clothing store increased the price of its suits by $7\frac{1}{2}\%$. What is the selling price of a suit that formerly sold for $226?

Method 1:

$7\frac{1}{2}\% = .075$

$226
x .075
1130
1582
$16.950

Method 2: Proportion Method

$$\frac{\text{mark - up}}{\text{original}} = \frac{\%}{100}$$

Substitute using: mark-up = n
original = 226
% = $7\frac{1}{2}$

$$\frac{n}{226} = \frac{7\frac{1}{2}}{100}$$

$$100n = 7\frac{1}{2} \times 226$$ Cross-multiply.

$$= \frac{15}{2} \times \frac{226}{1}$$

$$= 1695$$

$$\frac{100n}{100} = \frac{1695}{100}$$ Divide by 100.

$$n = \$16.95$$ This represents the amount of the mark-up.

Add the mark-up to the original price.

$226.00
+ 16.95
$242.95

The new price of the suit would be $241.95.

Finding the percent of increase or decrease

Use: $\dfrac{\text{change}}{\text{original}} = \dfrac{\%}{100}$

You must subtract the given quantities to determine the change.

Example 18

Coffee which normally sells for \$3.50 a pound was on sale for \$3.00 a pound. Find to the nearest tenth of a percent the percent of decrease in the price of a pound of coffee.

$$\frac{\text{change}}{\text{original}} = \frac{\%}{100}$$

Subtract to determine the change.

$$\frac{.50}{3.50} = \frac{n}{100}$$

Substitute using: change = .50
                    original = 3.50
                    % = n

$$\frac{3.50n}{3.50} = \frac{50}{3.50}$$

Cross-multiply and divide by 3.50.

n = 14.3% (to the nearest tenth)

The price of a pound of coffee decreased by approximately 14.3%.

Example 19

The price of a gallon of premium gasoline rose 10¢ a gallon to \$1.25. Find, to the nearest percent, the percent of increase in the price of a gallon of premium gasoline.

$$\frac{\text{change}}{\text{original}} = \frac{\%}{100}$$

The change is already given as .10.

$$\frac{.10}{1.15} = \frac{n}{100}$$

Substitute using: change = .10
                    original = 1.15
                    % = n

$$\frac{1.15n}{1.15} = \frac{10}{1.15}$$

Cross-multiply and divide by 1.15.

n = 9% (to the nearest percent)

The price of a gallon of premium gasoline rose approximately 9%.

Exercises

1. Change each percent to a fraction or mixed number in simplest form.
   (a) 13%
   (b) 7%
   (c) 40%
   (d) 125%
   (e) 100%
   (f) 1%
   (g) $4\frac{1}{3}\%$
   (h) $12\frac{1}{2}\%$
   (i) $7\frac{3}{4}\%$
   (j) $10\frac{2}{7}\%$
   (k) $\frac{4}{5}\%$
   (l) $8\frac{1}{4}\%$

2. Change each percent to a decimal number.
   (a) 3.5%
   (b) .035%
   (c) 52.76%
   (d) 83%
   (e) 8%
   (f) 800%
   (g) $5\frac{1}{2}\%$
   (h) $15\frac{1}{4}\%$
   (i) $\frac{3}{4}\%$
   (j) $81\frac{1}{5}\%$
   (k) $\frac{4}{5}\%$
   (l) $8\frac{1}{4}\%$

3. Change each number into a percent.
   (a) 12.3
   (b) 4
   (c) $\frac{4}{5}$
   (d) $7\frac{1}{2}$
   (e) $.05\frac{3}{4}$
   (f) $\frac{2}{3}$
   (g) .07
   (h) 30
   (i) $4\frac{1}{4}$
   (j) 1
   (k) .001
   (l) 6.008

4. Applications

(a) Find 8% of $152.

(b) $87\frac{1}{2}\%$ of what number is 56?

(c) 40 is what percent of 250?

(d) An oat bran muffin recipe calls for 3 ounces of low fat margarine and 9 ounces of other ingredients. What percent of the muffin is margarine?

(e) The purchase of a new $18,500 mini-van requires a down payment of 15%. How much is required for a down payment?

(f) A walkman is on sale for $35.00. The sign at the store reads "All Walkmans 30% Off - Today Only!" What was the original price of the walkman? [Hint: If you are getting 30% off, you are paying 70%.]

(g) Two competitive banks are advertising the following interest rates on their 12 month CD's:
   Royal Bank...10%

   Unity Bank...$9\frac{3}{4}\%$

How much additional interest would you receive on a $10,000 deposit by depositing your money into a 12 month CD at the Royal Bank rather than the Unity Bank?

(h) The 1988 IRS Tax Table states that married people filing jointly should pay $16,264.50 + 33% of the amount over $71,900 of your adjusted gross income. How much tax would Mr. and Mrs. Henderson pay on an adjusted gross income of $74,327 if they file jointly?

(i) Maria received a $3.60 tip from a customer, when waiting on his table. The total bill, without the tip, was $12. What percent of the total bill was left as a tip?

(j) The price of a gallon of gasoline rose from $1.10 to $1.25. What was the percent of increase (to the nearest percent)?

(k) A $65 dress is discounted by 20%. What is the sale price?

(l) The cost of a share of stock in a local utility company dropped from $12 to $9 a share. What is the percent of decrease in the cost of a share of this stock?

Answers

1. (a) $\frac{13}{100}$;   (b) $\frac{7}{100}$;   (c) $\frac{2}{5}$;   (d) $1\frac{1}{4}$;   (e) 1;

   (f) $\frac{1}{100}$;   (g) $\frac{13}{300}$;   (h) $\frac{1}{8}$;   (i) $\frac{31}{400}$;   (j) $\frac{18}{175}$;

   (k) $\frac{1}{125}$;   (l) $\frac{33}{400}$

2. (a) .035;   (b) .00035;   (c) .5276;   (d) .83;   (e) .08;
   (f) 8;   (g) .055;   (h) .1525;   (i) .0075;   (j) .812;
   (k) .008;   (l) .0825

3. (a) 1230%;   (b) 400%;   (c) 80%;   (d) 750%;   (e) $5\frac{3}{4}$%;

   (f) $66\frac{2}{3}$%;   (g) 7%;   (h) 3000%;   (i) 425%;   (j) 100%;

   (k) .1%;   (l) 600.8%

4. (a) $12.16;   (b) 64;   (c) 16%;   (d) 25%;   (e) $2775;
   (f) $50;   (g) $25;   (h) $17,065.41;   (i) 30%;   (j) 14%;
   (k) $52;   (l) 25%

GRAPHS

Graphs are pictures that represent data. A graph is usually more understandable than a table of numbers, and therefore more useful to us for purposes of comparison. We will cover three types of graphs: bar graphs, line graphs (sometimes called broken line graphs), and circle graphs.

Bar graphs

The height (or length) of each bar represents a given number (or given piece of data). As such, a bar graph is very useful when comparing data. The bars may be either vertical or horizontal.

Example 1

The graph below indicates how many newspapers Brian sold each day of a given week.

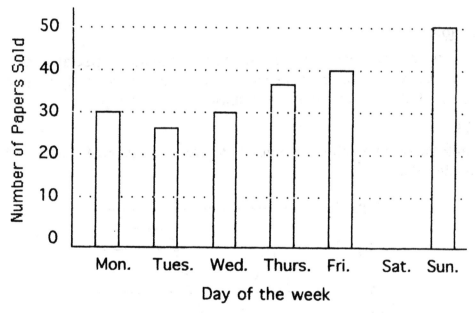

(a) On which day did he sell the most newspapers?
   Sunday -- since the bar representing Sunday has the greatest height.

(b) On which day might Brian have been home sick?
   Saturday -- since he did not sell any newspapers on Saturday.

(c) Approximately how many papers did Brian sell for the entire week?

Monday	30
Tuesday	25
Wednesday	30
Thursday	35
Friday	40
Saturday	0
Sunday	50
	210 newspapers

Brian sold approximately 210 newspapers for the entire week.

(d) What is the ratio of newspapers sold Monday to the total delivered by Brian for the week?

$$\frac{Monday}{Total} \quad \frac{30}{210} = \frac{1}{7}$$

Remember to reduce. Here, $\frac{30}{210}$ reduces to $\frac{1}{7}$ by dividing the numerator and denominator by 30.

Line Graphs

Line graphs are very useful as an indicator of change, especially in successive events. If the graph rises, it shows that the quantity is increasing. If the graph falls, it shows that the quantity is decreasing.

Example 2

The graph below indicates Carmen's test grades on each of 5 tests in her mathematics class.

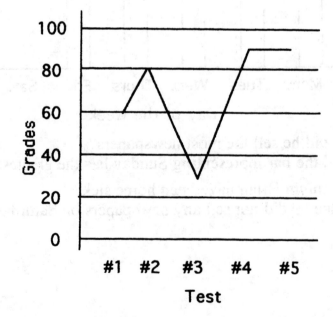

(a) Which test score shows that Carmen might not have studied enough? What was her score on that test?

Test #3 -- since she received a very low grade on that test. Her score was 30%.

(b) Between which two tests did Carmen show the most improvement?

Between test #3 and test #4, since this represents the greatest rise in the graph.

(c) Between which two tests did Carmen show no change in test scores?

Between test #4 and test #5 since she received 90% on each of these tests. Note that the line is horizontal between these two test scores.

(d) What was Carmen's average for the 5 tests?

Test #1 - 60
Test #2 - 80
Test #3 - 30
Test #4 - 90
Test #5 - 90
     350

$$\frac{70}{5)\overline{350}}$$

Remember: To find the average, you add up all the scores and divide by how many scores you have.

Carmen attained a 70% average on her 5 mathematics tests.

Circle graphs

Circle graphs are useful in showing the relationship between a specific quantity and the total. This is often done using percentages.

Example 3

The graph below indicates the Barnett family's monthly budget. The total monthly take-home pay is $2000.

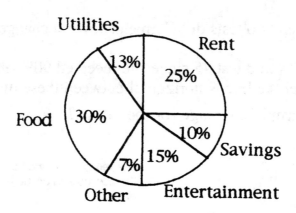

(a) Complete the table below

Barnett Family's Monthly Budget

Expenditure	% of total	Dollar amount budgeted
Rent	25%	$500 ($2000 x .25 = $500)
	10%	
Entertainment		
Utilities	13%	
	30%	
Other		

Barnett Family's Monthly Budget

Expenditure	% of total	Dollar amount budgeted
Rent	25%	$500 ($2000 x .25 = $500)
Savings	10%	$200 ($2000 x .10 = $200)
Entertainment	15%	$300 ($2000 x .15 = $300)
Utilities	13%	$260 ($2000 x .13 = $260)
Food	30%	$600 ($2000 x .30 = $600)
Other	7%	$140 ($2000 x .07 = $140)
Total	100%	$2000

(b) How much more was budgeted for entertainment than for utilities?

Using the completed table:
Entertainment $300
Utilities   -260
           $ 40

(c) How much additional must be budgeted for food if it is to represent 50% of the total take-home pay?

$2000
x .50
$1000

Take 50% of $2000.

$1000
- 600
$ 400

Subtract the amount budgeted for food ($600.)

An additional $400 would have to be budgeted for food in order for this to represent 50% of the total take-home pay.

Exercises

1. The graph below indicates the approximate rainfall in a mid-western US. town for six consecutive years.

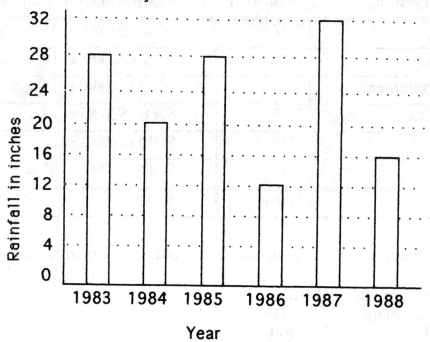

(a) Which year was the wettest?

(b) What was the difference in the amount of rainfall between 1984 and 1987?

(c) What was the average rainfall for the six years to the nearest inch?

(d) What is the ratio of rainfall in 1986 to that in 1983? (Simplify your answer.)

(e) Which years had the same amount of rainfall?

2. A car manufacturer claims that a car must have a "break-in" period before you can determine its true gas mileage. The graph below indicates the number of miles per gallon attained by a new convertible for its first five fill-ups.

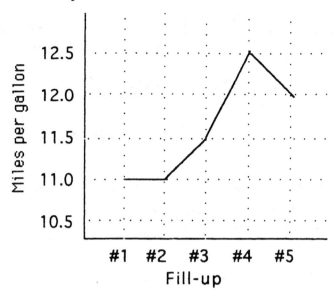

(a) Would you say the manufacturer is correct in their claim regarding gas mileage? Explain.

(b) The greatest increase occurred between which two fill-ups?

(c) What was the difference in the miles per gallon from the first to the fifth fill-ups?

(d) During which two fill-ups was there no change in miles per gallon?

(e) What was the average miles per gallon for the five fill-ups?

3. A diet center limited the calorie intake of one of its members to 1200 calories per day. The graph below indicates the daily calorie intake per food group for this member.

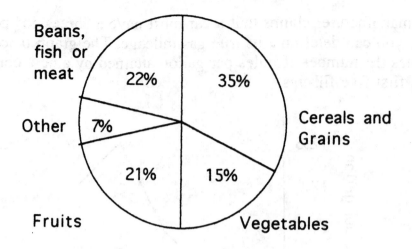

Beans, fish or meat — 22%
Cereals and Grains — 35%
Other — 7%
Fruits — 21%
Vegetables — 15%

(a) How many calories are allowed for beans, fish or meat?

(b) If the member increases the fruit intake to 25%, by how many calories must the "Other" category be decreased in order to not exceed the 1200 calorie limit?

(c) How many more calories are allowed for fruit than for vegetables?

(d) How many calories are allowed for fruits, vegetables, cereals and grains, and other?

(e) The dieter has an ice cream containing 250 calories. By how much does this exceed the allowable "Other" intake?

4. A video store wishes to maintain a proper balance of types of video tapes for its customers. the graph below indicates the number of video tapes it has available according to type in its 500 title collection.

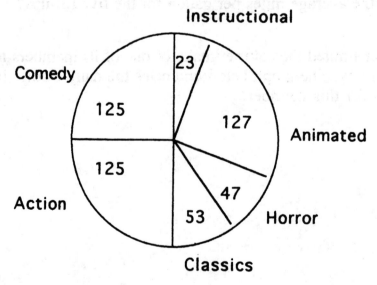

Instructional — 23
Comedy — 125
Animated — 127
Action — 125
Horror — 47
Classics — 53

(a) Comedy and action tapes represent what percent of the total?

(b) How many more classic tapes are there as compared to instructional tapes?

(c) What is the ratio of comedy tapes to action tapes?

(d) If an additional 100 comedy tapes are purchased, comedy would represent what percent of the total?

(e) How many classic tapes must be added to match the total of horror and instructional tapes?

5. The graph below indicates the batting average of a baseball player playing Triple A ball over the past five years.

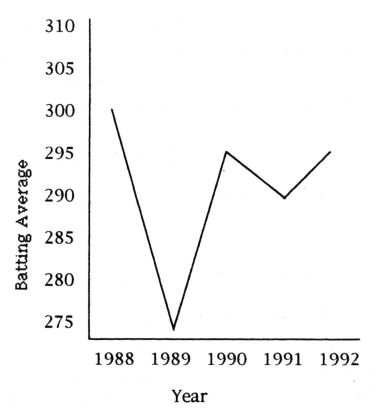

(a) Which year represents his best achievement?

(b) In which year would you say he was in a slump?

(c) During which years was his batting average the same?

(d) Between which two years did his batting average decline the most?

(e) What is the average of his batting average for the five years?

6. The graph below represents the time spent by Donna studying for each of her courses on a typical night.

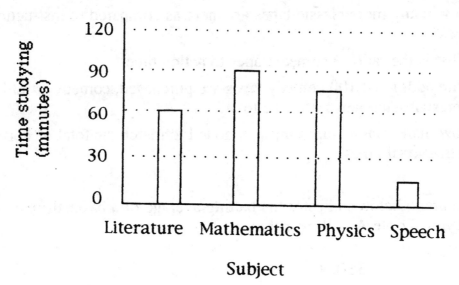

Subject

(a) How many hours does Donna spend studying on a typical night?

(b) How much more time is spent studying mathematics than speech?

(c) What is the ratio of time spent studying physics to time spent studying mathematics?

(d) The time spent studying literature represents what percent of the total study time?

(e) Which course seems to require the most studying?

Answers

1. (a) 1987   (b) 12 inches   (c) 23 inches   (d) $\frac{3}{7}$ (e) 1983 & 1985

2. (a) Yes, since the number of miles per gallon increased significantly after the "break-in" period.

   (b) The third and fourth.   (c) 1 mile per gallon

   (d) The first and second.   (e) 11.6 miles per gallon

3. (a) 264 calories   (b) 48 calories   (c) 72 calories   (d) 936 calories

   (e) 166 calories

4. (a) 50%   (b) 30   (c) $\frac{1}{1}$ (d) 37.5%   (e) 17

5. (a) 1988   (b) 1989   (c) 1990, 1992   (d) 1988, 1989   (e) 291

6. (a) 4 hours   (b) 1 hour 15 minutes   (c) $\frac{5}{6}$ (d) 25%   (e) Mathematics

2. Further Algebraic Practice

SIGNED NUMBERS

I. <u>Mixed Singles</u>:

1. -15 + 6   2. -7 + 11

3. 8 - 13   4. - 20 - 5

5. (- 6)(- 8)   6. - 2(- 11)

7. - 5(- 4)   8. - 17 - 7

9. $\dfrac{-5}{5}$ 10. 3(- 5)

11. -4 + (- 4)   12. - 2(- 8)

13. - 17 + 24   14. $\dfrac{-6}{-3}$

15. (2)(- 2)(0)(+ 3)   16. - 8 - 10

17. 6 - 10   18. (- 12) + 5

19. $\dfrac{0}{-5}$ 20. $(-3)^4$

21. - 9 - (- 9)   22. - 16 - (- 2)

23. $(-3)^2$ 24. - 6 + (- 7)

25. (- 9) ÷ (- 3)   26. $(-1)^8$

27. -9 - 9   28. - 2(- 3)(- 4)

29. - 6 + 6   30. 6 - 11

31. -2^2 32. - 16 + (- 2)

33. $\dfrac{18}{-6}$ 34. $\dfrac{7}{0}$

35. - 5 - 6   36. 12 - 5

37. $(-2)^2$ 38. -1^8

39. $\dfrac{5}{0}$ 40. 12- (-1)

41. 5 + (- 2)   42. 3 - (- 8)

43. - 3 + 4   44. $\dfrac{-12}{-4}$

45. $15 + (-3)$

46. $15(-3)$

47. $-15 - (-3)$

48. $-15(-3)$

49. $-2(3)(-4)$

50. $-2(-3)(-5)$

51. -5^2

52. $(-5)^2$

53. $(-3)^3$

54. $-(-4)^3$

55. $-(-5)^2$

56. -10^2

57. $-(2)^5$

58. $-(-1)^4$

59. -3^3

60. $-(8)^2$

II. Mixed Operations:

1. $3(-5) + 7$

2. $-2(-8) - 5$

3. $3 + 5(7)$

4. $-(-5)^2 + \dfrac{7 - 8}{-1}$

5. $-3 - 5(2)$

6. $8(-4)(0) - 16$

7. $4(3) - 3(2)$

8. $(-32) + (-32)$

9. $3^2 - (3)^2$

10. $3(9 - 6)^2$

11. $4(6 - 2) - 3$

12. $4(2 - 3) + 5$

13. $2(5 - 7) + 6$

14. $5(2^3 - 3^2)$

15. $5 + 7(5 - 8)$

16. $-4(4 - 8)(3)$

17. $3(2 + 4) - 3^2$

18. $\dfrac{2^2 - 5}{(-1)^2} + 7$

19. $3 + 5(6 - 8)$

20. $-8 + (-7)(+3)$

21. $-3(-5)(-1)$

22. $15 - (-15)(-1)$

23. $5(-2) + \dfrac{6 - 2}{2}$

24. $(-3)^2 - 3^2$

25. $2^3 - 4(3 - 5)$

26. $4(5 - 9)^2 + 3$

27. $\dfrac{3 + 5}{4} - (-7)(-2)$

28. $\dfrac{18}{6} - (-3)$

29. $5 - (+3)(-4)$

30. $3(2)(-5)(0)(17)$

31. $\dfrac{4 + 8}{3} + 3^2$

32. $5(-7) + \dfrac{0}{(15)^2}$

33. $2 - (-2)^3$

34. $2(-5)(4 - 6)(3)$

35. $-2(-2)^3$

36. $-(-2)^4$

39. $2^5 - (2)^3$ 40. $(2)^3(2)^2$

III. <u>Evaluate</u> if a = 3, b = 2, c = 4, and d = -1
1. 5a   2. 7b
3. 3c   4. a + b
5. c + d   6. a - d
7. 2b - c   8. 4ab

9. $2b^2$ 10. $\dfrac{a + d}{b}$

11. $\dfrac{a - b}{2}$ 12. $c^2 - a^2$

13. $c^2 + d^2$ 14. $b^2 - 4d$
15. c - bd   16. $a^2 - d^2$
17. $c^2 - d^2$ 18. $4bd - a^2$
19. $d^2 - c^2$ 20. $d^2 - 3ad$

Answers

I.

1. - 9	2. 4	3. - 5	4. - 25
5. 48	6. 22	7. 20	8. - 24
9. - 1	10. - 15	11. - 8	12. 16
13. 7	14. 2	15. 0	16. - 18
17. - 4	18. - 7	19. 0	20. 81
21. 0	22. - 14	23. 9	24. - 13
25. 3	26. 1	27. - 18	28. - 24
29. 0	30. - 5	31. - 4	32. - 18
33. - 3	34. undefined	35. - 11	36. 7
37. 4	38. - 1	39. undefined	40. 13
41. 3	42. 11	43. 1	44. 3
45. 12	46. - 45	47. - 12	48. 45
49. 24	50. - 30	51. - 25	52. 25
53. - 27	54. 64	55. - 25	56. - 100
57. - 32	58. - 1	59. - 27	60. - 64

II.

1. - 8	2. 11	3. 38	4. - 24

5. - 13	6. - 16	7. 6	8. - 64
9. 0	10. 27	11. 13	12. 1
13. 2	14. - 5	15. - 16	16. 48
17. 9	18. 6	19. - 7	20. - 29
21. - 15	22. 0	23. - 8	24. 0
25. - 16	26. 67	27. - 12	28. 6
29. 17	30. 0	31. 13	32. - 35
33. 10	34. 60	35. 16	36. - 16
37. - 16	38. 7	39. 24	40. 32

III.

1. 15	2. 14	3. 12	4. 5
5. 3	6. 4	7. 0	8. 24
9. 8	10. 1	11. $\frac{1}{2}$	12. 7
13. 17	14. 8	15. 6	16. 8
17. 15	18. - 17	19. - 15	20. 10

EVALUATING ALGEBRAIC EXPRESSIONS-- APPLIED PROBLEMS

The formula for the **perimeter of a rectangle** *is* $P = 2L + 2W$, *where* P *is the perimeter,* L *is the length, and* W *is the width. Use this formula for problems 1 - 4.*

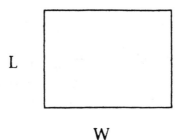

1. Find the perimeter of a rectangle when the length is 2 m and the width is 3 m.

2. Find the perimeter of a rectangle when the length is 21 cm and the width is 15 cm.

3. A rectangular shaped pool needs to be fenced in. How many meters of fencing must be purchased if the outer edge of the walk around the pool is 60 m long and 25 m wide.

4. Trim is to be purchased to go along the edges of a rectangular shaped table. If the table is 2.5 ft by 3.2 ft, how many feet of trim must be purchased?

The **area of a rectangle** *is determined by the formula* $A = LW$ *where* A *is the area,* L *is the length, and* W *is the width. Use this formula for problems 5 - 8.*

5. Find the area for a rectangle that is 12 cm long and 16 cm wide.

6. If the length of a rectangle is $2\frac{1}{2}$ in and the width is $\frac{3}{4}$ in, find the area of the rectangle.

7. What is the area of a rug that measures 9 ft long and 12 ft wide?

8. A gallon of paint covers a surface area of 400 sq ft. A room has two walls 20 ft long and 8 ft high, and two walls 12 ft long and 8 ft high. If you do not have to paint the doorway (3 ft side, 7 ft high) and the two windows (3 ft wide, 6 ft high) how much paint should you buy?

The formula for the **Area of a traingle** *is* $A = \frac{1}{2}bh$ *where* b *is the base of the triangle and* h *is the height. Use the formula to solve problems 9 - 12.*

9. Find the area of a triangle with height of 20 in and a base of 30 in.

10. Find the area of a triangle with a height of 2.3 cm and a base of 4.1 cm.

11. Find the area of a triangle with a base of $1\frac{1}{2}$ ft and a height of $2\frac{1}{2}$ ft.

12 A machine part is shaped like a triangle with a small hole in the center. The base of the triangle is 10.3 cm and the height is 5.1 cm. Find the remaining area if the hole cut out in the center has an area of 2.51 sq cm.

The formula for **distance travelled** *is* **d = rt**, *where* d *is the distance,* r *is the rate, and* t *is the time. Use the formula for problems 13 - 15.*

13. How far does a car travel when it goes 35 mi/hr for 3 hrs?

14. What is the destance travelled by a plane travelling at 450 mi/hr for 2.5 hrs?

15. What is the distance covered by a bicyclist going 20 mi/hr for $\frac{1}{2}$ hr?

The formula for **temperature conversion** *from degrees Farenheit to degrees Celsius is* $C = \frac{5}{9}$ **(F-32)**, *where* C *is for degrees Celsius and* F *is for degrees Farenheit. Use this formula for problems 16 - 18.*

16. Find the Celsius equivalent to 32°F.

17. Find the Celsius equivalent to 212°F.

18. Find the Celsius equivalent to 98.6°F.

The formula for the **Area of a trapezoid** *is* $A = \frac{1}{2}h(B + b)$, *where* B *and* b *are the parallel bases,* h *is the height (perpendicular distance between the bases). Use the formula for problems 19 and 20.*

19. Find the area of a trapezoid with bases measuring 4 cm and 6 cm, and a height of 5 cm.

20. Find the area of a trapezoid with bases measuring 2.3 cm and 3.8 cm, and a height of 5 cm.

Answers

1. 10 m	2. 72 cm	3. 170 m	4. 11.4 ft
5. 192 sq cm	6. $1\frac{7}{8}$ sq in	7. 108 sq ft	8. 1 gal and 1 qt or 2 gal
9. 300 sq in	10. 4.715 sq cm	11. $\frac{15}{8}$ or $1\frac{7}{8}$ sq ft	12. 23.755 sq cm
13. 105 mi	14. 1,125 mi	15. 10 mi	16. 0°C
17. 100°C	18. 37°C	19. 25 sq cm	20. 15.25 sq cm

TRANSLATING ALGEBRAIC EXPRESSIONS

1. 8 more than k

2. The sum of m and n

3. The total of $\frac{4}{5}$ and b

4. 1.25 increased by x

5. The difference between 6 and k

6. Subtract 18 from m

7. $4\frac{1}{2}$ less than D

8. W decreased by t

9. The product of -2.7 and n

10. One fourth of p

11. j times k

12 Twice y

13. -45 divided by x

14. The quotient of a and .25

15. The ratio of b to c

16. k squared

17. m cubed

18. 5 more than t

19. 5 more than twice t

20. 5 more than t cubed

21. 5 less than t

22. 5 less than the product of t and 7

23. 6 less than the product of t and $\frac{4}{5}$

24. 6 less than the quotient of t and .8

25. 6 more than the difference between t and .8

26. 6 less than the difference between t and .8

27. The difference between 18 and the product of t and 9

28. The difference between 18 and the quotient of t and 10

29. The difference between -12 and the cube of x

30. The sum of 16 and the square of y

31. The sum of $\frac{3}{4}$ and $\frac{2}{5}$ of x

32. The product of 1.75 and the square of g

33. The product of -2.03 and the sum of x and 2

34. The product of 8 and the difference of x and y

35. The quotient of 144 and the difference of y and z

36. The quotient of a and the cube of b

37. Four fifths of the sum of x and y

38. 3 less than the quotient of x and .06

39. .6 less than the product of p and q

40. Twice the sum of 5 and v

41. 18 more than an unknown number

42. The sum of 16 and a number

43. The total of .3 and a number

44. $\frac{7}{8}$ increased by a number

45. The difference between an unknown quantity and 4

46. Subtract $2\frac{2}{3}$ from a number

47. 8 decreased by a number

48. The product of 2.03 and an unknown number

49. Seven eighths of a number

50. Twice a number

51. The quotient of an unknown number and 17

52. A number divided by -6

53. The ratio of 7 and an unknown quantity

54. 3 more than a number

55. 5 more than twice a number

56. 8 more than a number cubed

57. 82 less than the product of a number and 3

58. $\frac{2}{3}$ of the sum of a number and 11

59. The product of 2.08 and the sum of a number and 1.3

60. the sum of a square of a number and twice the number

61. the difference of a cube of a number and the number

62. 5 less than the total of a number and 6

63. 16 less than the product of a number and one-half

64. One third of the sum of a number and 8

65. Four fifths of the difference of 8 and an unknown number

66. Twice the sum of the square of a number and 16

67. The value of d dimes

68. The value of q quarters

69. The value of n nickels

70. The total value of p pennies and n nickels

71. The total value of n nickels and q quarters

72. The total value of q quarters and d dimes

73. The cost of g gallons of water at 3 dollars each

74. The cost of k kites at 6 dollars each

75. The cost of p pairs of shoes at $50 a pair

76. The cost of p pizzas for $9 each and b bottles of soda for $2 each

77. The cost of m yards of material for $1.15 a yard and r yards of ribbon for $2.35 a yard

78. The cost of b dozen bagels for $3.17 a dozen and r dozen rolls for $1.08 a dozen

Answers

1. k + 8;

2. m + n;

3. $\frac{4}{5}$ + b;

4. 1.25 + x;

5. 6 - k;

6. m - 18;

7. D - $4\frac{1}{2}$;

8. w - t;

9. -2.7n;

10. $\frac{1}{4}$p;

11. jk;

12. 2y;

13. $\frac{-45}{x}$;

14. $\frac{a}{.25}$;

15. b:c or $\frac{b}{c}$;

16. k^2;

17. m^3;

18. t + 5;

19. 2t + 5;

20. t^3 + 5;

21. t - 5;

22. 7t - 5;

23. $\frac{4}{5}$t - 6;

24. $\frac{t}{.8}$ - 6;

25. $(t - .8) + 6$;   26. $(t - .8) - 6$;   27. $18 - 9t$;   28. $18 - \dfrac{t}{10}$;

29. $-12 - x^3$;   30. $16 + y^2$;   31. $\dfrac{3}{4} + \dfrac{2}{5}x$;   32. $1.75g^2$;

33. $-2.03(x + 2)$;   34. $8(x - y)$;   35. $\dfrac{144}{y - z}$;   36. $\dfrac{a}{b^3}$;

37. $\dfrac{4}{5}(x + y)$;   38. $\dfrac{x}{.06} - 3$;   39. $pq - .6$;   40. $2(5 + v)$;

41. $n + 18$;   42. $16 + n$;   43. $.3 + n$;   44. $\dfrac{7}{8} + x$;

45. $y - 4$;   46. $x - 2\dfrac{2}{3}$;   47. $8 - n$;   48. $2.03y$;

49. $\dfrac{7}{8}x$;   50. $2n$;   51. $\dfrac{m}{17}$;   52. $\dfrac{n}{-6}$;

53. $\dfrac{7}{x}$ or $7 : x$;   54. $n + 3$;   55. $2x + 5$;   56. $n^3 + 8$;

57. $3x - 82$;   58. $\dfrac{2}{3}(x + 11)$;   59. $2.08(n + 1.3)$;   60. $x^2 + 2x$;

61. $n^3 - n$;   62. $(x + 6) - 5$;   63. $\dfrac{1}{2}n - 16$;   64. $\dfrac{1}{3}(x + 8)$;

65. $\dfrac{4}{5}(8 - x)$;   66. $2(x^2 + 16)$;   67. $10d$;   68. $25q$;

69. $5n$;   70. $p + 5n$;   71. $5n + 25q$;   72. $25q + 10d$;

73. $\$3g$;   74. $\$6k$;   75. $\$50p$;   76. $\$9p + \$2b$;

77. $\$1.15m + \$2.35r$;   78. $\$3.17b + \$1.08r$

WORD PROBLEMS FOR LINEAR EQUATIONS WITH ONE UNKNOWN

1. Five more than a number is 61. Find the number.

2. Eleven less than a number is 15. Find the number.

3. A number decreased by 7 is 43. Find the number.

4. The sum of a number and -15 is -21. Find the number.

5. The product of 4 and a number is 4000. Find the number.

6. Twice a number is -44. Find the number.

7. 16 less than a number is -20. Find the number.

8. A number divided by -9 is -54. Find the number.

9. The result when a number is divided by 300 is -30. Find the number.

10. Nine less than a number is 0. Find the number.

11. Six less than twice a number is 42. Find the number.

12. Eight more than three times a number is -49. Find the number.

13. Four more than twice a number is 14 times the same number. Find the number.

14. 18 less than 5 times a number is 3 times the same number. Find the number.

15. If you add 8 to the product of a number and 9, the result is 98. Find the number.

16. If you subtract 6 from the sum of a number and 11, the result is 71. Find the number.

17. 3 times the sum of a number and 8 is 5 times the same number. Find the number.

18. Twice the difference between a number and 18 is equal to 58. Find the number.

19. 5 times the difference between a number and 5 is 80 times the same number. Find the number.

20. The product of -8 and the sum of a number and 2 equals 62. Find the number.

21. The product of 10 and the sum of a number and 201 equals 4 times the same number. Find the number.

22. The sum of a number and 3 times the number is equal to 812. Find the number.

23. The difference between a number and 3 times the number equals -16. Find the number.

24. Five times the sum of an unknown number and 8 equals 60. Find the number.

25. Five times the sum of an unknown number and 81 equals 2 times the unknown number. Find the number.

26. A salesperson earned $32,000 this year. If this was $5000 more than last year, how much did the salesperson earn last year?

27. The value of a house is $200,000. If this is 4 times the value of the house 10 years ago, how much was the house worth 10 years ago?

28. An antique vase sold for $8000 at an auction. This was $5000 more than the seller originally paid for it? How much did the seller originally pay for the vase?

29. A used press costs $1200. This is three-fifths of the cost of a new press. What is the cost of a new press?

30. Textbooks last semester cost one student $128. This is $16 less than the cost this semester. What is the cost of the books this semester?

31. The population of a summer resort town is 12,000. This is 6 times the population of the town during the winter. What is the population of the town during the winter?

32. One number is four less than a second number. the sum of the larger number plus twice the smaller number is 28. Find the numbers.

33. One number is five times a second number. The difference between the larger number and the smaller number is 16. Find the two numbers.

34. One number is 10 more than a second number. Four times the larger number minus three times the smaller number equals 33. Find the numbers.

35. One number is 1 more than twice a second number. The sum of the numbers is 10. Find the numbers.

36. One number is 1 less than three times a second number. The sum of the numbers is 19. Find the numbers.

37. One number is 3 less than another. Twice the sum of the numbers is negative thirty. Find the numbers.

38. One number is 2 more than three times a second number. the difference of the numbers is 14. Find the numbers.

39. One number is 5 less than twice another number. The sum of the two numbers is 70. Find the numbers.

40. One number is three-fourths of another. Twice the smaller number equals 12 more than the larger number. Find the numbers.

41. The perimeter of a rectangle is 20 cm. The length is four cm more than the width.

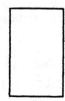

   Find the dimensions.

42. The perimeter of a rectangle is 40 m. The width is 3 times the length. Find the dimensions.

43. The perimeter of a rectangle is 104 yds. The width is 10 yds less than the length. Find the dimensions.

44. The perimeter of a rectangle is 52 mm. The width is 4 mm less than the length. Find the dimensions.

45. The perimeter of a rectangle is 270 ft. The length is 10 ft more than 4 times the width. Find the dimensions.

46. The perimeter of a rectangle is 160 km. The length is 8 km less than 3 times the width. Find the length.

47. The perimeter of a rectangle is 44 in. The length is 2 in more than four times the width. Find the width.

48. The perimeter of a rectangle is 2200 cm. The width is 100 cm less than half the length. Find the dimensions.

49. The perimeter of a triangle is 10 m. The second side is 1 m more than the first side. The third side is 3 m more than the first side.

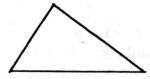

Find the dimensions.

50. The perimeter of a triangle is 24 cm. The first side is 3 cm less than the second side. The third side is 3 cm more than the second side. Find the dimensions.

51. The perimeter of a triangle is 41 mm. the first side is 9 mm less than the second side. The third side is 5 mm more than the second side. Find the dimensions.

52. The perimeter of a triangle is 13 yds. The second side is 1 yd more than the first side. The third side is double the first side. Find the dimensions.

53. The perimeter of a triangle is 41 km. The first side is 3 km less than the second side. The third side is 2 km more than the second side. Find the dimensions.

54. The perimeter of an isosceles triangle is 7 ft. The base is 1 ft more than the length of the equal sides. Find the dimensions.

55. The perimeter of an isosceles triangle is 15 in. The equal sides are each 3 in less than the base. Find the length of the equal sides.

56. A 24 ft board is cut into two pieces. One piece is 4 ft longer than the other. Find the length of each piece.

57. A 72 ft board is cut into two pieces. One piece is twice as long as the other. Find the length of each piece.

58. A 28 m strip of metal is cut into two pieces. One piece is 3 times as long as the other. Find the length of each piece.

59. A 16 yd piece of material is cut into two pieces. One piece is one yd longer than twice the length of the other. Find the length of each piece.

60. A 43 acre parcel of land is divided into 2 parcels. One parcel is 2 acres less than twice the size of the other parcel. Find the size of each parcel.

61. A fire department received an average of 30 calls a day over a three-day period. If they received 30 calls the first day and 42 calls the second day, how many calls were received the third day?

62. A student received 72, 95 and 85 on three exams. If the student wants an 85 average in the course, what must the student score on the fourth exam?

63. The price of a certain stock averaged 118 over three days. If the stock sold for 103 and 124 the first two days, what was its price on the third day?

64. A weight loss program advertised that the five customers pictured lost an average of 15 pounds on its program. If the first four pictured lost 6, 10, 14 and 17 pounds, how much did the fifth person lose?

Answers

1. 56;   2. 26;   3. 50;   4. -6;
5. 1000;   6. -22;   7. -4;   8. 486;
9. -9000;   10. 9;   11. 24;   12. -19;
13. $\frac{1}{3}$;   14. 9;   15. 10;   16. 66;

17. 12;   18. 47;   19. $\frac{-1}{3}$;   20. $-9\frac{3}{4}$;
21. -335;   22. 203;   23. 8;   24. 4;
25 -135;   26. $27,000;   27. $50,000;   28. $3000;
29. $2000;   30. $144;   31. 2000;   32. 8 and 12;
33. 4 and 20;   34. -7 and 3;   35. 3 and 7;   36. 5 and 14;
37. -6 and -9;   38. 6 and 20;   39. 25 and 45;   40. 18 and 24;
41. 3 cm and 7 cm;   42. 5 m and 15 m;
43. 21 yds and 31 yds;   44. 11 mm and 15 mm;

45. 25 ft and 110 ft;   46. 22 km   47. 4 in
48. 300 cm and 800 cm;   49. 2 m, 3 m, 5 m;
50. 5 cm, 8 cm, 11 cm;   51. 6 mm, 15 mm, 20 mm;

52. 3 yds, 4 yds, 6 yds;   53. 11 km, 14 km, 16 km;

54. 2 ft, 2 ft, 3 ft;   55. 4 in   56. 10 ft, 14 ft;
57. 24 ft, 48 ft;   58. 7 m, 21 m;
59. 5 yd, 11 yd;   60. 15 acres, 28 acres;
61. 18;   62. 88;   63. 127;   64. 28 lbs

REWRITING FORMULAS

Solve for the indicated variable.

1. $V = abc$ (for c)

2. $E = IR$ (for I)

3. $W = kEI$ (for k)

4. $PV = nRT$ (for R)

5. $D = \dfrac{W}{V}$ (for W)

6. $D = \dfrac{N}{P}$ (for P)

7. $D = \dfrac{N}{P}$ (for N)

8. $S = \dfrac{WL}{4Z}$ (for W)

9. $S = \dfrac{MC}{I}$ (for M)

10. $W = \dfrac{kE^2}{Z}$ (for Z)

11. $PV = nRT$ (for R)

12. $P = A + B + C$ (for A)

13. $F = \dfrac{Gm_1 m_2}{s^2}$ (for m_1)

14. $D = \dfrac{kI^2 t}{A}$ (for t)

15. $PV = nRT$ (for n)

16. $E = \dfrac{F}{A}$ (for A)

17. $P = \dfrac{FL}{TC}$ (for T)

18. $P = S - c$ (for c)

19. $F = \dfrac{Wv^2}{gR}$ (for R)

20. $2a = d_1 + d_2$ (for a)

21. $r = \dfrac{C - t}{n}$ (for C)

22. $v_1 - v_0 = at$ (for v_0)

23. $D = \dfrac{n + N}{2C}$ (for n)

24. $A + B + C = 360$ (for A)

25. $O = I^2 R - P$ (for R)

26. $W = RI^2 t$ (for R)

27. $M = \dfrac{q}{p}$ (for p)

28. $P = \dfrac{FL - d}{N}$ (for d)

29. $\dfrac{F_1}{a_1} = \dfrac{F_2}{a_2}$ (for a_1)

30. $P = \dfrac{Gd^4 F}{8ND^3}$ (for N)

Solve for y:

31. $3x + y = 10$

32. $5x + y = 3$

33. $-2x + y = -4$

34. $9x + y = -1$

35. x + y -3 = 0   36. 2x + y + 4 = 0

37. -2x - y = 21   38. 3x - y = -8

39. x - y - 32 = 0   40. -x - y - 9 = 0

41. x + 2y = 7   42. 3x - 5y = 6

43. 6x - 5y = 2   44. -7x - 3y = 5

45. 2x - 3y + 5 = 0   46. -3x +2y - 8 = 0

47. x + 4y - 21 = 0   48. x - 7y - 7 = 0

49. 3x + 3y = 21   50. 5x + 5y = -15

51. 12x - 3y = -6   52. -40x + 8y = 8

53. -56 = 8x - 7y   54. 35 = 5x + 7y

Answers

1. $c = \dfrac{V}{ab}$; 2. $I = \dfrac{E}{R}$; 3. $k = \dfrac{W}{EI}$; 4. $R = \dfrac{PV}{nT}$;

5. W = DV; 6. $P = \dfrac{N}{D}$; 7. N = DP; 8. $W = \dfrac{4SZ}{L}$;

9. $M = \dfrac{SI}{C}$; 10. $Z = \dfrac{kE^2}{W}$; 11. $R = \dfrac{PV}{nT}$; 12. A = P - B - C;

13. $m_1 = \dfrac{Fs^2}{Gm_2}$; 14. $t = \dfrac{AD}{kI^2}$; 15. $n = \dfrac{PV}{RT}$; 16. $A = \dfrac{F}{E}$;

17. $T = \dfrac{FL}{CP}$; 18. c = S - p; 19. $R = \dfrac{Wv^2}{Fg}$; 20. $a = \dfrac{d_1 + d_2}{2}$;

21. C = nr + t; 22. $v_0 = v_1 - at$; 23. n = 2CD - N; 24. A = 360 - B - C;

25. $R = \dfrac{O + P}{I^2}$; 26. $R = \dfrac{W}{I^2t}$; 27. $p = \dfrac{q}{M}$; 28. d = FL - NP;

29. $a_1 = \dfrac{a_2 F_1}{F_2}$; 30. $N = \dfrac{Gd^4F}{8D^3P}$; 31. y = 10 - 3x; 32. y = 3 - 5x;

33. y = 2x - 4; 34. y = - 9x - 1; 35. y = 3 - x; 36. y = - 2x - 4;

37. y = -2x - 21; 38. y = 3x + 8; 39. y = x - 32; 40. y = -x - 9;

41. $y = \dfrac{7 - x}{2}$; 42. $y = \dfrac{3x - 6}{5}$ 43. $y = \dfrac{6x - 2}{5}$; 44. $y = \dfrac{7x + 5}{-3}$;

or $y = \dfrac{6 - 3x}{- 5}$; or $y = \dfrac{-7x - 5}{3}$

45. $y = \dfrac{2x + 5}{3}$; 46. $y = \dfrac{3x + 8}{2}$ 47. $y = \dfrac{-x + 21}{4}$; 48. $y = \dfrac{x - 7}{7}$ or

or $y = \dfrac{3}{2}x + 4$; $y = \dfrac{1}{7}x - 1$;

49. y = -x + 7; 50. y = -x - 3; 51. y = 4x + 2; 52. y = 5x + 1;

53. $y = \dfrac{8}{7}x + 8$; 54. $y = - \dfrac{5}{7}x + 5$

SIMPLIFYING POLYNOMIAL EXPRESSIONS

Multiply and combine like terms.

1. $3(a + 5) + 7(a - 6)$
2. $(4x^2 - 3x + 5) - (-2x^2 + 7x - 5)$
3. $4a^2(-3ab) - 2a^3(b + 3)$
4. $y(y + 2) - 4(y^2 - 7)$
5. $(8x^3 + 5x^2 - 4) - (6x^2 + 4x - 3)$
6. $7a - 4b - 2(4a - 3b)$
7. $xy(3x^2 - 2y^2) - 2xy(2x^2 - y^2)$
8. $ab(7a - 3c) - bc(2a - b)$
9. $z(z - 3) - z(z + 4) - 9z$
10. $a^2 + 2a^2(3b) - (-3a^2) - 6b(a^2)$
11. $8x(xy^2) + 3xy(xy) - 2x^2y^2$
12. $(r - 2s + 3t) - (4r + s - t) + (-3r - 2s)$
13. $4x^2y^3(-3xy) - 7(x^3y^4 + 2) + 3xy(-4x^2y^3)$
14. $5ab^2 - 3(2ab^2 + 4)$
15. $-5a(a^2 - 2a + 5) - 3a(4a^2 - 8) + (-3)(+5)$
16. $4x^2y^2(2x - 3y - 5) - 12x^3y^2 - 4x^2y^3$
17. $3y^2 - 5(y^2 + 3y - 7) - 3y(y + 6) - (-6y)$
18. $-r^3(t) - t(-4r^3)$
19. $3x + 5x(x + 5) - (2x - 6)$
20. $(5 - x)4 - 3(2x - 5) + (3x - 6)$
21. $-(5x^2 + 3x + 10) + (7x^2 - 6) - (-3)$
22. $5(3y^3 - 2y^2 + 7y - 8) - 4(-6y^3 + 7y - 1)$
23. $8 - 5(3u + 3) - (5u + 3) + (-5)$
24. $3x^2(4x^2 - 3x) - (-2x^3 - 7) + 4(x^4)$
25. $(5 - a) + 7(a + 4) - 3(a + 5)$
26. $(x + 3)^2 - 2x$
27. $(3xy^2)^2 + xy^2 - x^2y^4$
28. $- (-5xy)^3 - 5xy$
29. $(3xy)^2 - (5x^2y)^3 + 5x^2y^2$

30. $(x - 2)^2 - (x-3)^2$

31. $(-3a^4b)^3 - (-3a^4b)^3$

32. $3(x - 2)^2 - 5(x + 4)^2$

Answers

1. $10a - 27$
2. $6x^2 - 10x + 10$
3. $-14a^3b - 6a^3$
4. $-3y^2 + 2y + 28$
5. $8x^3 - x^2 - 4x - 1$
6. $-a + 2b$
7. $-x^3y$
8. $7a^2b - 5abc + b^2c$
9. $-16z$
10. $4a^2$
11. $9x^2y^2$
12. $-6r - 5s + 4t$
13. $-31x^3y^4 - 14$
14. $-ab^2 - 12$
15. $-17a^3 + 10a^2 - a - 15$
16. $-4x^3y^2 - 16x^2y^3 - 20x^2y^2$
17. $-5y^2 - 27y + 35$
18. $3r^3t$
19. $5x^2 + 26x + 6$
20. $-7x + 29$
21. $2x^2 - 3x - 13$
22. $39y^3 - 10y^2 + 7y - 36$
23. $-20u - 15$
24. $16x^4 - 7x^3 + 7$
25. $3a + 18$
26. $x^2 + 4x + 9$
27. $8x^2y^4 + xy^2$
28. $125x^3y^3 - 5xy$
29. $-125x^6y^3 + 14x^2y^2$
30. $2x - 5$
31. 0
32. $-2x2 - 52x - 68$

MIXED FACTORING

Factor the following expressions completely:

1. $x^2 - 5x - 6$
2. $x^2 - 64$
3. $5k^2 - 25k$
4. $y^2 - 2y - 15$
5. $a^2 - 14a + 49$
6. $3m^3 - 9m^2$
7. $y^2 + 1$
8. $y^2 - 1$
9. $45x - 9$
10. $x^8 - x^7$
11. $x^2 - x - 20$
12. $10a^2 - 100a$
13. $y^2 + y - 42$
14. $y^2 - 121$
15. $8a^2 - 4a$
16. $15x^2 - 20x$
17. $30q - 45$
18. $7x^3 - 15x^2$
19. $12ax - 15ay$
20. $2x^3 - 2x$
21. $x^2y - 9y$
22. $3y^2 - 12$
23. $6x^2 - 60x + 150$
24. $16x^2y - 4y$
25. $x^2 - 6x - 16$
26. $50x^2 - 30x$
27. $5x^4 - 10x^3$
28. $x^2 - 11x - 42$
29. $4x^2 + 64x + 252$
30. $x^2y^2 - xy^3 - y^4$

Answers

1. $(x - 6)(x + 1)$;
2. $(x - 8)(x + 8)$;
3. $5k(k - 5)$;
4. $(y - 5)(y + 3)$;
5. $(a - 7)^2$;
6. $3m^2(m - 3)$;
7. not factorable;
8. $(y - 1)(y + 1)$;
9. $9(5x - 1)$;
10. $x^7(x - 1)$;
11. $(x - 5)(x + 4)$;
12. $10a(a - 10)$;
13. $(y + 7)(y - 6)$;
14. $(y - 11)(y + 11)$;
15. $4a(2a - 1)$;
16. $5x(3x - 4)$;
17. $15(2q - 3)$;
18. $x^2(7x - 15)$;
19. $3a(4x - 5y)$;
20. $2x(x - 1)(x + 1)$;
21. $y(x - 3)(x + 3)$;
22. $3(y - 2)(y + 2)$;
23. $6(x - 5)^2$;
24. $4y(2x - 1)(2x + 1)$;
25. $(x + 2)(x - 8)$;
26. $10x(5x - 3)$;
27. $5x^3(x - 2)$;
28. $(x - 14)(x + 3)$;
29. $4(x + 9)(x + 7)$;
30. $y^2(x^2 - xy - y^2)$

QUADRATIC EQUATIONS

Solve the following equations:

1. $y^2 + 2y + 1 = 0$

2. $2x^2 - 32 = 0$

3. $25p^2 - 64 = 0$

4. $6r^2 - 60r = 0$

5. $2y^2 - 6y - 8 = 0$

6. $s^2 - 13s + 42 = 0$

7. $z^2 - 4z - 96 = 0$

8. $8x^2 - 8 = 0$

9. $4b^2 - 100 = 0$

10. $4w^2 - 25 = 0$

11. $25x^2 - 16 = 0$

12. $3y^2 - 9y - 30 = 0$

13. $a^2 + a = 0$

14. $5x^2 + 10x - 15 = 0$

15. $100b^2 - 81 = 0$

16. $p^2 - 2p = 0$

17. $x^2 + 4x = 0$

18. $x^2 + 6x + 5 = 0$

19. $u^2 - 4u - 77 = 0$

20. $49y^2 - 1 = 0$

21. $y^2 - 2y - 35 = 0$

22. $x^2 - 8x + 7 = 0$

23. $t^2 + 2t - 35 = 0$

24. $4r^2 - 8r = 0$

25. $x^2 + 2x - 63 = 0$

26. $3x^2 - 27 = 0$

27. $a^2 - 14a + 49 = 0$

28. $5x^2 - 45 = 0$

29. $4x^2 - 4x - 48 = 0$

30. $2y^2 - 10y - 12 = 0$

31. $12x^2 - 48x + 48 = 0$

32. $x^2 - 7x + 12 = 0$

33. $z^2 - 2z = 0$

34. $r^2 - 49 = 0$

35. $3a^2 + 18a + 27 = 0$

36. $d^2 - 14d + 13 = 0$

37. $7x^2 - 63 = 0$

38. $3t^2 - 75 = 0$

39. $x^3 - x = 0$

40. $a^2 + 3a - 10 = 0$

41. $15w^2 - 10w = 0$

42. $3b^2 - 48 = 0$

43. $2x^3 + 4x^2 - 6x = 0$

44. $x^2 - x - 90 = 0$

45. $y^2 - 54 = -3y$

46. $49n^2 = 36$

47. $x^2 - 12x = -32$

48. $3x^2 + 24x = -45$

49. $y^2 + 6y = -8$

50. $5z^2 = 15z$

Answers

1. $y = -1$, $y = -1$

2. $x = 4$, $x = -4$

3. $p = \frac{8}{5}$, $p = -\frac{8}{5}$

4. $r = 0$, $r = 10$

5. $y = 4$, $y = -1$

6. $s = 7$, $s = 6$

7. $z = 12$, $z = -8$

8. $x = 1$. $x = -1$

9. $b = 5$, $b = -5$

10. $w = \frac{5}{2}$, $w = -\frac{5}{2}$

11. $x = \frac{4}{5}$, $x = -\frac{4}{5}$

12. $y = 5$, $y = -2$

13. $a = 0$, $a = -1$

14. $x = -3$, $x = 1$

15. $b = \frac{9}{10}$, $b = -\frac{9}{10}$

16. $p = 0$, $p = 2$

17. $x = 0$, $x = -4$

18. $x = -5$, $x = -1$

19. $u = 11$, $u = -7$

20. $y = \frac{1}{7}$, $y = -\frac{1}{7}$

21. $y = 7$, $y = -5$

22. $x = 7$, $x = 1$

23. $t = -7$, $t = 5$

24. $r = 0$, $r = 2$

25. $x = -9$, $x = 7$

26. $x = 3$, $x = -3$

27. $a = 7$, $a = 7$

28. $x = 3$, $x = -3$

29. $x = 4$, $x = -3$

30. $y = 6$, $y = -1$

31. $x = 2$, $x = 2$

32. $x = 4$, $x = 3$

33. $z = 0$. $z = 2$

34. $r = 7$, $r = -7$

35. $a = -3$, $a = -3$

36. $d = 13$, $d = 1$

37. $x = 3$, $x = -3$

38. $t = 5$, $t = -5$

39. $x = 0$, $x = 1$, $x = -1$

40. $a = -5$, $a = 2$

41. $w = 0$, $w = \frac{2}{3}$

42. $b = 4$, $b = -4$

43. $x = 0$, $x = 1$, $x = -3$

44. $x = 10$, $x = -9$

45. $y = -9$, $y = 6$

46. $n = \frac{6}{7}$, $n = -\frac{6}{7}$

47. $x = 8$, $x = 4$

48. $x = -5$, $x = -3$

49. $y = -4$, $y = -2$

50. $z = 0$, $z = 3$

MULTIPLICATION AND DIVISION OF ALGEBRAIC FRACTIONS

Simplify:

1. $\dfrac{56}{45} \cdot \dfrac{81}{49}$

2. $\dfrac{xy}{z} \cdot \dfrac{z}{xy}$

3. $\dfrac{m^2}{m} \cdot \dfrac{n}{n^2}$

4. $\dfrac{x^3}{y^4} \cdot \dfrac{z^2}{y^3} \cdot \dfrac{x^2}{z}$

5. $\dfrac{-3y}{6x^2} \cdot \dfrac{4x^3}{-y}$

6. $\dfrac{26a^3}{25b} \cdot \dfrac{5}{3a^2} \cdot \dfrac{-5b}{13a}$

7. $\dfrac{-24ab^2}{8a} \cdot \dfrac{21a^2b}{14b}$

8. $3x^4y^4 \cdot \dfrac{1}{9x^5y^2}$

9. $\dfrac{-56r^2s^3t}{24rs^2t^3} \cdot \dfrac{-48t}{28rst}$

10. $\dfrac{6m^2}{5n^2} \cdot \dfrac{10mn}{-6m^3}$

11. $\dfrac{24x^3y^2}{-7z^3} \cdot \dfrac{21z^2}{12xy}$

12. $\dfrac{1}{3x^4y^4} \cdot \dfrac{-12x^5}{5y^2}$

13. $\dfrac{-4xy^2}{-3x^3} \cdot \dfrac{6x^5y}{-8xy^5}$

16. $\dfrac{8}{12} \div \dfrac{16}{32}$

17. $\dfrac{3}{6y} \div \dfrac{3}{9y}$

18. $\dfrac{ab^2}{a^2b} \div \dfrac{a}{b^3}$

19. $\dfrac{x^2}{y^3} \div \dfrac{-x^3}{y^2}$

20. $\dfrac{6m^2n^2}{-8p^2} \div 3mn$

21. $\dfrac{7y^3}{3y^3} \div \dfrac{6y^2}{21y}$

22. $\dfrac{-u^2v^2}{r^2t^2} \div \dfrac{uv^2}{r^2t}$

23. $\dfrac{36x^4}{5y^2} \div \left(-4x^3\right)$

24. $\dfrac{8x^2y^2}{12xy} \div \dfrac{6x^3}{-4y^4}$

25. $\dfrac{16d^3}{21c^2} \div \dfrac{24d^2}{14c^2}$

26. $\dfrac{-4pq^2}{15p^3} \div \dfrac{-16q^3}{25pq}$

27. $\dfrac{2xy^2}{5x^2} \div \dfrac{1}{25xy^3}$

28. $\dfrac{5pq^2}{-10q} \div 10q$

14. $\dfrac{2r^2s^3}{-5rs^3} \cdot \dfrac{-4r^2s}{10s^4}$

15. $\dfrac{-t^3v^2}{-12t^5} \cdot \dfrac{3tv}{-8v^4}$

29. $-2xy^2 \div \dfrac{1}{-6x^2y^3}$

30. $\dfrac{-5a^2bc^3}{3a^3b} \div \dfrac{10ab^4}{-6c^2}$

Answers

1. $\dfrac{72}{35} = 2\dfrac{2}{35}$

2. 1

3. $\dfrac{m}{n}$

4. $\dfrac{x^5z}{y^7}$

5. $2x$

6. $-\dfrac{2}{3}$

7. $-\dfrac{9a^2b^2}{2}$

8. $\dfrac{y^2}{3x}$

9. $\dfrac{4}{t^2}$

10. $-\dfrac{2}{n}$

11. $-\dfrac{6x^2y}{z}$

12. $\dfrac{-4x}{5y^6}$

13. $-\dfrac{x^2}{y^2}$

14. $\dfrac{4r^3}{25s^3}$

15. $-\dfrac{1}{32tv}$

16. $\dfrac{4}{3} = 1\dfrac{1}{3}$

17. $\dfrac{3}{2} = 1\dfrac{1}{2}$

18. $\dfrac{b^4}{a^2}$

19. $-\dfrac{1}{xy}$

20. $-\dfrac{mn}{4p^2}$

21. $\dfrac{49}{6y}$

22. $-\dfrac{u}{t}$

23. $-\dfrac{9x}{5y^2}$

24. $-\dfrac{4y^5}{9x^2}$

25. $\dfrac{4d}{9}$

26. $\dfrac{5}{12p}$

27. $10y^5$

28. $\dfrac{-p}{20}$

29. $12x^3y^5$

30. $\dfrac{c^5}{a^2b^4}$

ADDITION AND SUBTRACTION OF LIKE ALGEBRAIC
FRACTIONS

Simplify:

1. $\dfrac{3}{x} + \dfrac{5}{x}$

2. $\dfrac{9}{16y} - \dfrac{7}{16y}$

3. $-\dfrac{6}{11k^3} - \dfrac{1}{11k^3}$

4. $-\dfrac{5}{9a^2} + \dfrac{7}{9a^2}$

5. $\dfrac{2}{5x} + \dfrac{18}{5x}$

6. $\dfrac{15}{2k} - \dfrac{11}{2k}$

7. $\dfrac{2y}{3} - \dfrac{5y}{3}$

8. $\dfrac{x}{9} + \dfrac{8x}{9}$

9. $\dfrac{2x}{3} - \dfrac{5}{3}$

10. $\dfrac{12a}{5} - \dfrac{9}{5}$

11. $\dfrac{3x}{8} - \dfrac{9x}{8}$

12. $-\dfrac{2k}{90} - \dfrac{7k}{90}$

13. $\dfrac{7x}{16} - \dfrac{x}{16}$

14. $-\dfrac{3y}{5y^2} - \dfrac{2y}{5y^2} -$

15. $-\dfrac{9y}{8y} + \dfrac{y}{8y}$

16. $\dfrac{14m}{25m} - \dfrac{9}{25m}$

17. $\dfrac{x+3}{8} + \dfrac{x+5}{8}$

18. $\dfrac{2y-1}{6} + \dfrac{3y-2}{6}$

19. $\dfrac{b+2}{9} + \dfrac{b-3}{9}$

20. $\dfrac{a-5}{6} - \dfrac{2a-1}{6}$

21. $\dfrac{3k+3}{2} - \dfrac{5k-2}{2}$

22. $\dfrac{7a-3}{6} - \dfrac{a+3}{6}$

23. $\dfrac{5x-2}{x} - \dfrac{3x-3}{x}$

24. $\dfrac{7b+3}{b} - \dfrac{9b-5}{b}$

Answers

1. $\dfrac{8}{x}$

2. $\dfrac{1}{8y}$

3. $\dfrac{-7}{11k^3}$

4. $\dfrac{2}{9a^2}$

5. $\dfrac{4}{x}$

6. $\dfrac{2}{k}$

7. $-y$

8. x

9. $\dfrac{2x-5}{3}$

10. $\dfrac{12a-9}{5}$

11. $-\dfrac{3x}{4}$

12. $-\dfrac{k}{10}$

13. $\dfrac{3x}{8}$

14. $-\dfrac{1}{y}$

15. -1

16. $\dfrac{14m-9}{25m}$

17. $\dfrac{x+4}{4}$

18. $\dfrac{5y-3}{6}$

19. $\dfrac{2b-1}{9}$

20. $\dfrac{-a-4}{6}$

21. $\dfrac{-2k+5}{2}$

22. $a-1$

23. $\dfrac{2x+1}{x}$

24. $\dfrac{-2b+8}{b}$

ADDITION AND SUBTRACTION OF UNLIKE ALGEBRAIC FRACTIONS

Simplify:

1. $\dfrac{3x}{5} - \dfrac{2x}{7}$

2. $\dfrac{2y}{3} + \dfrac{3y}{5}$

3. $-\dfrac{9a}{7} - \dfrac{a}{8}$

4. $-\dfrac{2a}{3} - \dfrac{5}{7}$

5. $\dfrac{7y}{5} + \dfrac{3}{8}$

6. $\dfrac{2x}{9} - \dfrac{5}{7}$

7. $\dfrac{a}{8} - \dfrac{3a}{4}$

8. $\dfrac{2y}{9} - \dfrac{5y}{3}$

9. $-\dfrac{x}{10} + \dfrac{3x}{5}$

10. $\dfrac{b}{2} - \dfrac{3b}{10}$

11. $\dfrac{r}{9} + \dfrac{r}{18}$

12. $\dfrac{z}{7} - \dfrac{5z}{21}$

13. $\dfrac{x}{3} - \dfrac{5}{12}$

14. $\dfrac{2}{7} + \dfrac{3a}{14}$

15. $-\dfrac{9y}{25} - \dfrac{6}{5}$

16. $\dfrac{3x}{4} + \dfrac{x}{6}$

17. $\dfrac{2a}{9} - \dfrac{a}{12}$

18. $\dfrac{5x}{14} - \dfrac{3x}{21}$

19. $-\dfrac{8a}{35} - \dfrac{5a}{21}$

20. $\dfrac{-7x}{27} + \dfrac{x}{18}$

21. $\dfrac{4y}{15} - \dfrac{9y}{20}$

22. $\dfrac{5x}{6} - \dfrac{6}{15}$

23. $\dfrac{3a}{35} + \dfrac{2}{15}$

24. $\dfrac{y}{12} - \dfrac{3}{4}$

25. $\dfrac{8x}{9} - \dfrac{8}{21}$

26. $\dfrac{5}{8} - \dfrac{3x}{6}$

27. $\dfrac{11}{30} - \dfrac{12x}{25}$

28. $8p - \dfrac{2}{5}$

29. $5 - \dfrac{5x}{7}$

30. $3y - \dfrac{4}{9}$

31. $\dfrac{1}{2} - 18k$

32. $\dfrac{3x}{2} + 7$

33. $\dfrac{2x}{5} + 11$

34. $\dfrac{5}{x} - \dfrac{3}{4}$

35. $-\dfrac{2}{y} + \dfrac{3}{7}$

36. $\dfrac{8}{9} - \dfrac{5}{k}$

37. $\dfrac{4}{7} - \dfrac{2}{y}$

38. $\dfrac{5}{9} + \dfrac{3}{k}$

39. $\dfrac{-8}{5} - \dfrac{5}{y}$

40. $\dfrac{3}{5} - \dfrac{2}{5y}$

41. $\dfrac{5}{8} + \dfrac{3}{8x}$

42. $-\dfrac{7}{9} - \dfrac{5}{9x}$

43. $\dfrac{-2}{3y} - \dfrac{5}{3}$

44. $\dfrac{8}{11a} - \dfrac{3}{11}$

45. $\dfrac{5}{2x} - \dfrac{3}{2}$

46. $\dfrac{3}{x} - \dfrac{2}{5x}$

47. $\dfrac{-7}{y} - \dfrac{3}{5y}$

48. $\dfrac{14}{3x} - \dfrac{5}{x}$

49. $\dfrac{-2}{7a} - \dfrac{3}{a}$

50. $\dfrac{4}{3m} + \dfrac{2}{m}$

51. $\dfrac{-4}{21a} + \dfrac{4}{a}$

52. $\dfrac{-3}{5x} + \dfrac{2}{3x}$

53. $\dfrac{8}{15y} - \dfrac{7}{10y}$

54. $\dfrac{-2}{9k} + \dfrac{8}{15k}$

55. $\dfrac{-5}{12y} + \dfrac{7}{16y}$

56. $\dfrac{2}{35r} - \dfrac{9}{14r}$

57. $\dfrac{11}{4x} + \dfrac{23}{6x}$

58. $\dfrac{3}{5a} - \dfrac{9}{10a}$

59. $-\dfrac{8}{3y} - \dfrac{5}{12y}$

60. $\dfrac{7}{8a} - \dfrac{3}{4a}$

61. $\dfrac{3}{4x} - \dfrac{5}{2}$

62. $\dfrac{7}{8} + \dfrac{9}{4y}$

63. $\dfrac{15}{8g} - \dfrac{5}{32}$

64. $\dfrac{-1}{7x} - \dfrac{5}{14}$

65. $\dfrac{-7}{18k} - \dfrac{1}{10}$

66. $\dfrac{3}{2} - \dfrac{5}{6y}$

67. $\dfrac{8}{m} + \dfrac{9}{n}$

68. $\dfrac{3x}{y} - \dfrac{2}{x}$

69. $\dfrac{5}{a} + \dfrac{2}{3b}$

70. $\dfrac{4a}{3b} - \dfrac{b}{9a}$

71. $\dfrac{5}{x} + \dfrac{2}{5y}$

72. $\dfrac{10}{3c} + \dfrac{5}{8d}$

73. $\dfrac{3}{x^2} - \dfrac{5}{x}$

74. $\dfrac{8}{y} + \dfrac{10}{y^2}$

75. $\dfrac{2a}{3b^2} - \dfrac{3a}{b}$

76. $\dfrac{6}{5k} + \dfrac{9}{10k^2}$

77. $\dfrac{3}{2b^2} - \dfrac{7}{8b}$

78. $\dfrac{4}{3y^2} + \dfrac{7}{2y^2}$

79. $\dfrac{5}{ab^2} + \dfrac{8}{a^2 b}$

80. $\dfrac{9}{x^3 y} - \dfrac{5}{x^2 y^2}$

81. $\dfrac{11}{mn^3} + \dfrac{3}{n^2}$

82. $\dfrac{9}{xy^3} + \dfrac{15}{y}$

83. $\dfrac{1}{x^4 y} + \dfrac{2}{x^5 y}$

84. $\dfrac{4}{a^2 b^4} + \dfrac{3}{ab^4}$

Answers

1. $\dfrac{11x}{35}$

2. $\dfrac{19y}{15}$

3. $\dfrac{-79a}{56}$

4. $\dfrac{-14a-15}{21}$

5. $\dfrac{56y+15}{40}$

6. $\dfrac{14x-45}{63}$

7. $\dfrac{-5a}{8}$

8. $\dfrac{-13y}{9}$

9. $\dfrac{x}{2}$

10. $\dfrac{b}{5}$

11. $\dfrac{r}{6}$

12. $\dfrac{-2z}{21}$

13. $\dfrac{4x-5}{12}$

14. $\dfrac{4+3a}{14}$

15. $\dfrac{-9y-30}{25}$

16. $\dfrac{11x}{12}$

17. $\dfrac{5a}{36}$

18. $\dfrac{3x}{14}$

19. $\dfrac{-49a}{105}$

20. $\dfrac{-11x}{54}$

21. $\dfrac{-11y}{60}$

22. $\dfrac{25x-12}{30}$

23. $\dfrac{9a+14}{105}$

24. $\dfrac{y-9}{12}$

25. $\dfrac{56x-24}{63}$

26. $\dfrac{5-4x}{8}$

27. $\dfrac{55-72x}{150}$

28. $\dfrac{40p-2}{5}$

29. $\dfrac{35-5x}{7}$

30. $\dfrac{27y-4}{9}$

31. $\dfrac{1-36k}{2}$

32. $\dfrac{3x+14}{2}$

33. $\dfrac{2x+55}{5}$

34. $\dfrac{20-3x}{4x}$

35. $\dfrac{-14+3y}{7y}$

36. $\dfrac{8k-45}{9k}$

37. $\dfrac{4y-14}{7y}$

38. $\dfrac{5k+27}{9k}$

39. $\dfrac{-8y-25}{5y}$

40. $\dfrac{3y-2}{5y}$

41. $\dfrac{5x+3}{8x}$

42. $\dfrac{-7x-5}{9x}$

43. $\dfrac{-2-5y}{3y}$

44. $\dfrac{8-3a}{11a}$

45. $\dfrac{5-3x}{2x}$

46. $\dfrac{13}{5x}$

47. $\dfrac{-38}{5y}$

48. $\dfrac{-1}{3x}$

49. $\dfrac{-23}{7a}$

50. $\dfrac{10}{3m}$

51. $\dfrac{80}{21a}$

52. $\dfrac{1}{15x}$

53. $\dfrac{-1}{6y}$

54. $\dfrac{14}{45k}$

55. $\dfrac{1}{48y}$

56. $\dfrac{-41}{70r}$

57. $\dfrac{79}{12x}$

58. $\dfrac{-3}{10a}$

59. $\dfrac{-37}{12y}$

60. $\dfrac{1}{8a}$

61. $\dfrac{3 - 10x}{4x}$

62. $\dfrac{7y + 18}{8y}$

63. $\dfrac{60 - 5g}{32g}$

64. $\dfrac{-2 - 5x}{14x}$

65. $\dfrac{-35 - 9k}{90k}$

66. $\dfrac{9y - 5}{6y}$

67. $\dfrac{8n + 9m}{mn}$

68. $\dfrac{3x^2 - 2y}{xy}$

69. $\dfrac{15b + 2a}{3ab}$

70. $\dfrac{12a^2 - b^2}{9ab}$

71. $\dfrac{25y + 2x}{5xy}$

72. $\dfrac{80d + 15c}{24cd}$

73. $\dfrac{3 - 5x}{x^2}$

74. $\dfrac{8y + 10}{y^2}$

75. $\dfrac{2a - 9ab}{3b^2}$

76. $\dfrac{12k + 9}{10k^2}$

77. $\dfrac{12 - 7b}{8b^2}$

78. $\dfrac{29}{6y^2}$

79. $\dfrac{5a + 8b}{a^2b^2}$

80. $\dfrac{9y - 5x}{x^3y^2}$

81. $\dfrac{11 + 3mn}{mn^3}$

82. $\dfrac{9 + 15xy^2}{xy^3}$

83. $\dfrac{x + 2}{x^5y}$

84. $\dfrac{4 + 3a}{a^2b^4}$

FRACTIONAL EQUATIONS

Solve:

1. $\dfrac{x}{2} + \dfrac{x}{3} + \dfrac{x}{4} = 13$

2. $\dfrac{3}{y} + \dfrac{1}{4} = \dfrac{1}{2y}$

3. $\dfrac{p}{5} = \dfrac{15}{25}$

4. $\dfrac{3}{7} = \dfrac{6}{a+8}$

5. $\dfrac{3x}{x+6} = 5$

6. $\dfrac{5}{6} - \dfrac{1}{3x} = 0$

7. $\dfrac{x-7}{9} - \dfrac{x}{4} = -3$

8. $\dfrac{2x}{3} - \dfrac{1}{5} = \dfrac{1}{3} + \dfrac{2x}{5}$

9. $\dfrac{2}{a+3} = \dfrac{5}{a}$

10. $\dfrac{5}{m+1} = \dfrac{15}{m+7}$

11. $\dfrac{2}{5} + \dfrac{y}{15} = \dfrac{1}{3}$

12. $\dfrac{5x}{8} - \dfrac{x}{3} = \dfrac{5x}{6} - 13$

13. $\dfrac{7t}{12} - \dfrac{1}{4} = 2t - \dfrac{5}{3}$

14. $1 = \dfrac{3x}{4} - \dfrac{2x}{3}$

15. $\dfrac{4}{r} - \dfrac{1}{2} = \dfrac{5}{12} - \dfrac{3}{2r}$

16. $\dfrac{2+y}{6y} = \dfrac{3}{5y} + \dfrac{1}{30}$

17. $\dfrac{b+12}{9} = \dfrac{b-9}{2}$

18. $\dfrac{3}{4} - \dfrac{1}{8x} = 0$

19. $\dfrac{2y}{3} = -21$

20. $\dfrac{2a}{3} - \dfrac{2a+5}{6} = \dfrac{1}{2}$

21. $\dfrac{4}{x} + \dfrac{5}{2} = \dfrac{4x+5}{2x} - \dfrac{2x-3}{5x}$

22. $\dfrac{15}{c} + \dfrac{9c-7}{c} = 10$

23. $\dfrac{2}{x+1} = \dfrac{1}{x-2}$

24. $\dfrac{2}{3y-1} = \dfrac{3}{4y+1}$

25. $\dfrac{5y-3}{7} = \dfrac{15y-2}{28}$

26. $\dfrac{-1}{x^2-x+2} = \dfrac{-1}{x^2+2x+3}$

27. $\dfrac{2x}{3} - \dfrac{1}{5} = \dfrac{1}{3} + \dfrac{2x}{5}$

28. $\dfrac{4}{5x} - \dfrac{7}{10x} = \dfrac{1}{10}$

29. $\dfrac{3}{4x} - \dfrac{2}{x} = \dfrac{5}{12}$

30. $1 - \dfrac{3+y}{2y} = \dfrac{3-y}{y}$

Answers

1. x = 12
2. y = - 10
3. p = 3
4. a = 6
5. x = -15
6. $x = \frac{2}{5}$
7. x = 16
8. x = 2
9. a = - 5
10. m = 2
11. y = - 1
12. x = 24
13. t = 1
14. x = 12
15. r = 6

16. y = 2
17. b = 15
18. $x = \frac{1}{6}$
19. $y = -31\frac{1}{2}$
20. a = 4
21. x = -1
22. c = 8
23. x = 5
24. y = 5
25. y = 2
26. $x = -\frac{1}{3}$
27. x = 2
28. x = 1
29. x = -3
16. y = 3

DECIMAL EQUATIONS

Solve. If the answer does not terminate, round the answer to the nearest tenth.

1. $.3x + .2 = .5$

2. $.5y - 3 = 7$

3. $2 - .3x = 1.1$

4. $1.4 = .2y + 4$

5. $5 - 8x = .8x + .6$

6. $4 + .2y = 2.7y - 3.5$

7. $2.3 + 5x = .7x + 10.9$

8. $3x - .7 = 2.7x - .4$

9. $.1x - .02 = .14x$

10. $4.7 - .03x = .59$

11. $.12x - .3 = .37x$

12. $.4y + .5 = .32$

13. $.35y + .9 = 7.9$

14. $.502 = 1.3 - .2y$

15. $.25x = .32$

16. $.08 = 2.5x$

17. $3.5 - .02y = .3$

18. $.7 + .28x = 1.23$

19. $5 = .37x$

20. $.12 = 12x - 1.2$

21. $.15x - .3 = 8x + 50$

22. $7.25x - 3 = 5.82x$

Solve. If the answer does not terminate, round the answer to the nearest hundredth.

23. $3.6x + 5.75 = .03x$

24. $.05 = .235 - .2x$

25. $1.57 - 2x = .038$

26. $.05x - .05 = .05$

27. $12 - .357x = .009$

28. $3 + .3x = .03x - .003$

29. $1.25x - 5.25 = 1.35x$

30. $.12 - .08x - .3 = 0$

Answers

1. $x = 1$

2. $y = 20$

3. $x = 3$

4. $y = -13$

5. $x = .5$

6. $y = 3$

7. $x = 2$

8. $x = 1$

9. $x = -.5$

10. $x = 137$

11. $x = -1.2$

12. $y = -0.45$

13. $y = 20$

14. $y = 3.99$

15. $x = 1.28$

16. $x = 0.032$

17. $y = 160$

18. $x \approx 1.9$

19. $x \approx 13.5$

20. $x = 0.11$

21. $x \approx -6.4$

22. $x \approx 2.1$

23. $x \approx -1.61$

24. $x \approx 0.93$

25. $x \approx 0.77$

26. $x = 2$

27. $x \approx 33.59$

28. $x \approx -11.12$

29. $x = -52.5$

30. $x = -2.25$

PYTHAGOREAN THEOREM

I. Solve for the indicated variable. (The answer may be left in simplest radical form except for radicands that are perfect squares.)

1. a = 3 and b = 4. Find c.

2. a = 5 and b = 12. Find c

3. a = 8 and c = 17. Find b.

4. b = 7 and c = 9. Find a.

5. a = 15 and c = 25. Find b.

6. b = 3 and c = 4. Find a.

7. a = 12 and c = 13. Find b.

8. a = 6 and b = 3. Find c

9. a = 9 and b = 12. Find c.

10. a = 10 and c = 20. Find b.

II. Find the value of x in each triangle.

1.

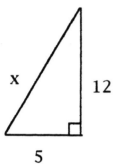

2.

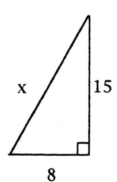

3.

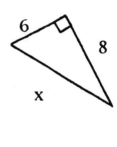

4.

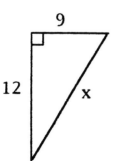

5.

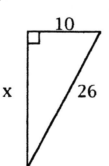

6.

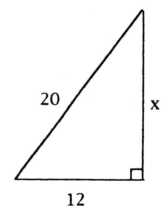

III. Applied Problems

1. The base of a 10 foot ladder is 6 feet away from a wall. How far off the ground is the top of the ladder?

2. Is a triangle whose sides are 6, 8 and 12 a right triangle?

3. Find the length of the sides of a square whose diagonal is 8 cm. (The answer may be left in simplest radical form.)

4. Find the length of the hypotenuse of a right triangle whose legs measure 4 and 5. (The answer may be left in simplest radical form.)

5. What is the length of a guide wire supporting a 30-foot antenna if the base of the guide wire is 16 feet from the base of the antenna?

Answers

I. Solve for the indicated variable.

1. $c = 5$ 2. $c = 13$ 3. $b = 15$ 4. $a = 4\sqrt{2}$ 5. $b = 20$

6. $a = \sqrt{7}$ 7. $b = 5$ 8. $c = 3\sqrt{5}$ 9. $c = 15$ 10. $b = 10\sqrt{3}$

II. Find the value of x in each triangle.

1. 13   2. 17   3. 10   4. 15   5. 24   6. 16

III Applied Problems

1. 8 feet

2. No. The sum of the squares of the legs does not equal the square of the hypotenuse.

3. $4\sqrt{2}$ cm

4. $\sqrt{41}$

5. 34 feet

3. Mathematics Skills Exam Preparation

PREPARING TO TAKE A MATHEMATICS SKILLS EXAM

This section contains some suggestions to help improve your chances of success on a mathematics skills exam and in your mathematics courses.

Weeks or months before the exam:

Take a practice test. Note what was wrong. Note what you get right by luck, what you get right by skill, what you feel you don't understand, what you feel you do understand.

Review, relearn or learn the mathematics you will be tested on. Give any topics that give you trouble extra time and attention. If you need to do extra problems to feel secure about a topic, the book and the supplement should provide you with what you need. There is no substitute for consciously doing the work needed to learn mathematics.

When you encounter an especially difficult, tricky, confusing, or noteworthy problem, write it on an index card. Work out the solution on the reverse. Save the cards. Before an exam, use the cards to create a self-test.

Be honest with yourself. If there is something you do not understand, ask a teacher or tutor about it before the exam. You will feel awful if you do not ask a question and then find it on the exam.

One week before the exam

Re-examine the topics that have been especially difficult. Do as many practice problems as you need to feel confident. Write yourself notes to explain how to identify these problems and/or how to proceed.

Take a sample exam under exam-like conditions (timed, uninterrupted, etc.). Correct the exam. Go back over any problem areas.

The night before the exam

Have a good night's sleep. If you need to memorize anything, sometimes it helps to look at it again before you go to sleep, but do not make yourself nervous or anxious.

The day of the exam

Eat a nourishing meal; your brain needs fuel.

Arrive at the exam room early. Bring the supplies you will need, such as sharp pencils, a sharpener, eraser, eye glasses.

The exam

Read the directions before beginning the exam.

Relax by breathing deeply a few times.

Make the best use of the time that is available. Do not spend too much time on topics that you know give you trouble; skip them and return later, after you have answered the problems you know you will do well on.

If all questions are worth the same number of points, do not spend too much time on any one question unless you have time to spare.

On multiple choice problems, try to eliminate unreasonable choices.

Practice Skills Exam A

1. Ninety million, three hundred five is written:
   (A) 90,305   (B) 9,305   (C) 90,305,000
   (D) 90,000,305   (E) 90,000,000,305

2. The average of 2, 7, 9, and 6 is
   (A) 6   (B) 24   (C) 4   (D) 12   (E) 18

3. 7 hours 5 minutes
   <u>-1 hour 45 minutes</u>

   (A) 6 hours 40 minutes   (B) 5 hours 15 minutes
   (C) 6 hours 20 minutes   (D) 5 hours 20 minutes
   (E) 5 hours 40 minutes

4. $11,368 \div 56$
   (A) 203   (B) 23   (C) 230   (D) 2003   (E) 2030

5. 503 - 89
   (A) 486   (B) 424   (C) 414   (D) 592   (E) 586

6. Which of the following fractions is the smallest?
   (A) $\frac{4}{5}$ (B) $\frac{7}{9}$ (C) $\frac{9}{10}$ (D) $\frac{5}{8}$ (E) $\frac{10}{9}$

7. A theater company sells 296 show tickets for $9 each. If the expenses for the show are $1200, how much money does the company make?
   (A) $2664   (B) $1464   (C) $1496   (D) $904   (E) $1004

8. $\frac{2}{5} + \frac{2}{9} =$
   (A) $\frac{28}{45}$ (B) $\frac{4}{45}$ (C) $\frac{4}{18}$ (D) $\frac{5}{14}$ (E) $\frac{4}{45}$

9. $8\frac{2}{5} - 6\frac{3}{5}$
   (A) $2\frac{1}{5}$ (B) $2\frac{4}{5}$ (C) $1\frac{2}{5}$ (D) $2\frac{2}{5}$ (E) $1\frac{4}{5}$

10. $4\frac{2}{5} \div 20$

(A) $\frac{11}{50}$ (B) 88   (C) $5\frac{2}{5}$ (D) $\frac{5}{2}$ (E) $\frac{440}{5}$

11. Which of the following numbers is <u>largest</u>?
(A) .0056   (B) .45   (C) .06   (D) .200   (E) .1000

12. .254 + 14 + 65.71 =
(A) 6.839   (B) 104.11   (C) 105.11   (D) 79.964   (E) 68.39

13. 12.9 - 4.56
(A) 16.46   (B) 3.27   (C) 8.46   (D) 17.46   (E) 8.34

14. Change $\frac{5}{9}$ to a decimal number rounded to the nearest hundredth.

(A) .56   (B) .55   (C) .59   (D) 5.9   (E) .556

15. Gasoline costs $.97 a gallon. If a tank holds 18 gallons of gasoline, how much does it cost to fill the tank?

(A) $1746   (B) $17.00   (C) $16.46   (D) $17.46   (E) $174.60

16. 60% of 90 is
(A) 54   (B) 60   (C) 5400   (D) 540   (E) 5.40

17. If 20% of a number is 256, what is the number?
(A) 1280   (B) 512   (C) 5120   (D) 12.8   (E) 51.2

18. If a coat sells for $80 and the tax is 8%, how much will you pay for the coat?

(A) $80.08   (B) $80.64   (C) $86.40   (D) $640   (E) $64

19. The graph below shows the number of cars sold at a dealership during the first four months of the year.

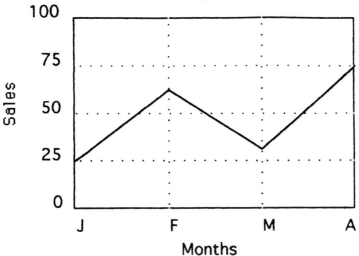

The difference in sales between the first month and the fourth month is:
(A) 3   (B) 75   (C) 50   (D) 100   (E) 25

20. The area of a rectangle with a length of 2" and a width of 8" is:
(A) 16"   (B) 20"   (C) 20 square inches   (D) 16 square inches
(E) 10"

21. The sum of 2x - 5y and - 5x + 6y is:
(A) - 3x + y   (B) 3x + y   (C) - 3x^2 + 1   (D) 3x - y
(E) - 3x^2 + y

22. The product of 8x^{3}y^2 and 7y is:
(A) 56x^{3}y^2 (B) 56x^{3}y^3 (C) 15x^{3}y^2 (D) 15x^{3}y^3
(E) 56x^3 + 7y^3

23. Simplify: $\dfrac{8y - 24}{8}$
(A) y - 24   (B) y - 16   (C) 8y - 3   (D) 8y + 3   (E) y - 3

24. Simplify: 5x^{3}y^2 - 4xy(2x^{2}y - 3)
(A) - 3x^{3}y^2 + 12xy   (B) - 3x^{3}y^2 - 3   (C) 13x^{4}y^3 (D) - 13x^{4}y^3
(E) 2x^{3}y^2 - x^{2}y

25. Add $3x^2 - 5x + 4$ and $-9x + 3$
   (A) $3x^2 + 14x + 7$ (B) $24x^3$ (C) $3x^2 - 14x + 7$ (D) $-11x^3 + 7$
   (E) $-6x^2 + 7$

26. $(3ab^4)^3$
   (A) $27a^3b^{12}$ (B) $9a^3b^7$ (C) $9a^3b^{12}$ (D) $27a^3b^7$
   (E) $9ab^{12}$

27. Factor: $8r^2 - 32r$
   (A) $-24r$ (B) $8r(r - 4)$ (C) $8r^2(-4)$ (D) $8(r - 4)$ (E) $-24r^2$

28. $(-5)^2 - 3(4)$
   (A) 28   (B) 52   (C) 88   (D) 13   (E) -37

29. If $3x - 8 = 52$, then $x =$
   (A) 20   (B) $\dfrac{44}{3}$ (C) 57   (D) -20   (E) $-\dfrac{44}{3}$

30. If $\dfrac{x}{6} = \dfrac{x}{4} - \dfrac{1}{3}$, then $x =$
   (A) 1   (B) -1   (C) 12   (D) 4   (E) -4

31. Which of the following points lies on the graph of $y = 6x - 2$?
   (A) (3,16)   (B) (10,2)   (C) (6,2)   (D) (3,-16)   (E) (2,6)

32. If red paint costs 9 dollars a quart and white paint costs 6 dollars a
   quart, how much will r quarts of red paint and w quarts of white paint
   cost?

   (A) rw dollars   (B) 54rw dollars   (C) 15rw dollars
   (D) 9r + 6w dollars   (E) 15(r + w) dollars

33. An equation for the line L on
   the right is:

   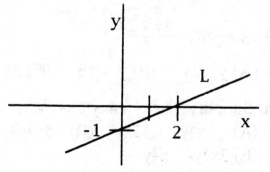

   (A) $y = -1$ (B) $x = 2$
   (C) $y = x - 1$ (D) $y = 2x - 1$
   (E) $y = \dfrac{1}{2}x - 1$

34. Find the value of P if x = 2 in the formula P = 10(5)^x.
    (A) 100   (B) 250   (C) 2500   (D) 320   (E) 20

35. If 4x - 3 = y, then x =
    (A) $\frac{y - 3}{4}$ (B) $\frac{y + 3}{4}$ (C) $\frac{-y}{4}$ (D) 3y - 4   (E) $\frac{y}{4}$ + 3

36. In the right triangle below, the length of the side labeled H is:

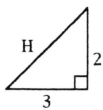

    (A) 4   (B) 5   (C) $6\frac{1}{2}$ (D) 13   (E) $\sqrt{13}$

37. If x - y = 3 and 2x + y = - 6, then
    (A) x = - 1, y = - 4   (B) x = - 1, y = 4   (C) x = 1, y = - 2
    (D) x = 1, y = - 4   (E) x = 3, y = 0

38. A survey showed that 4 out of 5 students in a certain course studied 6 hours or more for the final exam. If 40 students studied 6 hours or more, how many students studied less than 6 hours?

    (A) 40   (B) 8   (C) 32   (D) 10   (E) 50

39. A square park is enclosed with 120 yards of fencing. The area of the park is:

    (A) 900 square yards   (B) 240 square yards   (C) 120 square yards
    (D) 3600 square yards   (E) 1600 square yards

40. A student has grades of 72, 88 and 70 on the first three tests in a course. What grade must the student receive on the fourth test to have an average of 80 for the four tests?

    (A) 95   (B) 80   (C) 100   (D) 90   (E) 85

Solutions for the Practice Skills Exam A with References

1. Ninety million, three hundred five is written 90,000,305
   Answer: D
   Reference: *Supplement.* Whole numbers, Writing a Number.

2. The average of 2, 7, 9 and 6 is $\dfrac{2 + 7 + 9 + 6}{4} = \dfrac{24}{4} = 6$

   Answer: A
   Reference: *Supplement.* Whole numbers, Averages.

3.   7 hours 5 minutes = 6 hours 65 minutes
   <u>-1 hour 45 minutes</u> = <u>1 hour 45 minutes</u>
                         5 hours 20 minutes

   Answer: D
   Reference: *Supplement.* Measurement.

4. $$\begin{array}{r} 203 \\ 56\overline{)11368} \\ \underline{-112} \\ 168 \\ \underline{-168} \end{array}$$

   Answer: A
   Reference: *Supplement.* Whole numbers, Division.

5. $\begin{array}{r} 503 \\ \underline{-89} \\ 414 \end{array}$

   Answer: C
   Reference: *Supplement.* Whole numbers, Subtraction.

6. $\dfrac{4}{5} = \dfrac{288}{360}$ $\dfrac{7}{9} = \dfrac{324}{360}$ $\dfrac{9}{10} = \dfrac{270}{360}$ $\dfrac{5}{8} = \dfrac{225}{360}$ $\dfrac{10}{9} = 1\dfrac{1}{9}$

Answer: D

Reference: *Text..* Appendix 1. Equivalent fractions; Finding the Least Common Denominator.
Or, change the fractions to decimal numbers and then compare. See *Supplement.*, Converting a fraction to a decimal number, Comparing decimal numbers.

7. Profit = Income - Expenses

The income comes from selling the tickets. 296 tickets are $9 each, or 296 x $9 = $2664 income.
The expenses are given in the problem: $1200.
Profit = $2664 - $1200 = $1464

Answer: B

Reference: *Supplement.* Whole numbers and Word Problems.

8. $\dfrac{2}{5} + \dfrac{2}{9}$

The LCD for 5 and 9 is 45.

$\dfrac{2}{5} = \dfrac{(9)2}{(9)5} = \dfrac{18}{45}$ $\dfrac{2}{9} = \dfrac{(5)2}{(5)9} = \dfrac{10}{45}$

$\dfrac{18}{45} + \dfrac{10}{45} = \dfrac{28}{45}$

Answer A

Reference: *Text*. Appendix 1 Adding Unlike Fractions.

9. $8\dfrac{2}{5} - 6\dfrac{3}{5} = 7\dfrac{7}{5} - 6\dfrac{3}{5}$

$\qquad\qquad = 1\dfrac{4}{5}$

Answer E

Reference: *Text*. Appendix 1 Adding or Subtracting Mixed Numbers.

10. $4\frac{2}{5} \div 20 = \frac{22}{5} \div \frac{20}{1}$

$$= \frac{22}{5} \times \frac{1}{20}$$

$$= \frac{\overset{11}{\cancel{22}} \times 1}{5 \times \cancel{20}}$$

$$= \frac{11}{50}$$

Answer A

Reference: *Text* . Appendix 1 Multiplying or Dividing Mixed Numbers.

11. .0056 = .0056

   .45   = .4500

   .06   = .0600

   .200 = .2000

   .1000 = .1000

The largest number is .4500

Answer B

Reference: *Supplement.* Comparing Decimal Numbers.

12.   .254

     14.000

  +65.710

    79.964

Answer D

Reference: *Supplement.* Adding Decimal Numbers.

13. 12.90

  - 4.56

   8.34

Answer E

Reference: *Supplement.* Subtracting Decimal Numbers.

14. $\dfrac{5}{9} = 5 \div 9$

$$\begin{array}{r} .555... \\ = 9\overline{)5.000} \\ \underline{4.5} \\ 50 \\ \underline{45} \end{array}$$

Round to the nearest hundredth .555... becomes .56

Answer A

Reference: *Supplement*. Changing a Fraction to a Decimal Number

15. Number of gallons x price for each gallon = 18 x $.97 = $17.46

Answer D

Reference: *Supplement* Multiplying Decimal Numbers.

16. 60% of 90 is

.60 x 90 = 54.00 = 54

Answer A

Reference: *Supplement*. Per Cents.

17. 20% of a number is 256

$.20 \times N = 256$

$N = \dfrac{256}{.20}$ OR

$N = 1280$

$\dfrac{20}{100} = \dfrac{256}{N}$

$20 \times N = 100 \times 256$

$20 \times N = 25600$

$N = \dfrac{25600}{20}$

$N = 1280$

Answer A

Reference: *Supplement*. Per Cents.

18. Find 8% of $80. Then add it to $80.

$$\begin{aligned} 8\% \times \$80 &= .08 \times \$80 \\ &= \$6.40 \end{aligned}$$

$80 + $6.40 = $86.40

Answer C

Reference: *Supplement*. Per Cents.

19. Sales in Month 4 = 75
    Sales in Month 1 = 25
    The difference is 75 - 25 = 50

    Answer C

    Reference: *Supplement*. Graphs.

20. Area of a rectangle = length x width
    $$= 2 \text{ inches} \times 8 \text{ inches}$$
    $$= 16 \text{ square inches}$$

    Answer D

    Reference: *Text*. Chapter 1, Section 1.6, Evaluating Algebraic Expressions. Also see *Supplement*. Evaluating Algebraic Expressions -- Applied Problems.

21. $(2x - 5y) + (-5x + 6y) = 2x - 5y - 5x + 6y$
    $$= -3x + y$$

    Answer A

    Reference: *Text*. Chapter 4, Section 4.2, Adding and Subtracting Polynomials.

22. $(8x^3y^2)(7y) = 56x^3y^3$

    Answer B

    Reference: *Text*. Chapter 1, Section 1.5, Multiplying Expressions; Chapter 4, Multiplying Monomials.

23. $\dfrac{8y - 24}{8} = \dfrac{8y}{8} - \dfrac{24}{8}$
    $$= y - 3$$

    Answer E

    Reference: *Text*. Chapter 4, Section 4.5, Dividing Polynomials.

24. $5x^3y^2 - 4xy(2x^2y - 3) = 5x^3y^2 - 8x^3y^2 + 12xy$
    $$= -3x^3y^2 + 12xy$$

    Answer A

    Reference: *Text*. Chapter 4, Section 4.3, Multiplying Polynomials.

25. $(3x^2 - 5x + 4) + (-9x + 3) = 3x^2 - 5x + 4 - 9x + 3$
$$= 3x^2 - 14x + 7$$

Answer C

Reference: *Text*. Chapter 4, Section 4.2, Adding and Subtracting Polynomials.

26. $(3ab^4)^3 = (3)^3(a)^3(b^4)^3$
$$= 27a^3b^{12}$$

Answer A

Reference: *Text*. Chapter 9, Section 9.1, Extending the Properties of Exponents.

27. $8r^2 - 32r$
The GCF is $8r$
$8r(r - 4)$

Answer B

Reference: *Text*. Chapter 5, Factoring - an introduction.

28. $(-5)^2 - 3(4)$
$(-5)(-5)$
$25 - 3(4)$
$25 - 12$
13

Answer D

Reference: *Text*. Chapter 1, Section 1.6, Evaluating Algebraic Expressions. Also see Chapter 2, Section 2.4, Multiplying Signed Numbers.

29. $3x - 8 = 52$
$3x - 8 + 8 = 52 + 8$
$3x = 60$
$x = 20$

Answer A

Reference: *Text*. Chapter 3, Section 3.4, Combining Rules to Solve Equations.

30. $\dfrac{x}{6} = \dfrac{x}{4} - \dfrac{1}{3}$

The LCD is 12.

$12 \cdot \dfrac{x}{6} = 12 \cdot \dfrac{x}{4} - 12 \cdot \dfrac{1}{3}$

$2x = 3x - 4$

$x = 4$

Answer D

Reference: *Text*. Chapter 6, Section 6.7, Equations Involving Fractions.

31. Check to see which ordered Pair (x,y) satisfies the equation.

(3,16)
$y = 6x - 2$
$16 = 6(3) - 2$
$16 = 18 - 2$
$16 = 16$
True

(10,2)
$y = 6x - 2$
$2 = 6(10) - 2$
$2 = 60 - 2$
$2 = 58$
Not true

(6,2)
$y = 6x - 2$
$2 = 6(6) - 2$
$2 = 36 - 2$
$2 = 34$
Not true

(3,- 16)
$y = 6x - 2$
$-16 = 6(3) - 2$
$-16 = 18 - 2$
$-16 = 16$
Not true

(2,6)
$y = 6x - 2$
$6 = 6(2) - 2$
$6 = 12 - 2$
$6 = 10$
Not true

Answer A

Reference: *Text* . Chapter 7, Sections 7.1, Solutions of Equations in Two Variables.

32. r quarts for $9 each is 9·r or 9r dollars.
    w quarts for $6 each is 6·w or 6w dollars.
    The total of 9r and 6w is 9r + 6w dollars.

Answer D

Reference: *Text*. Chapter 1, Section 1.1, From Arithmetic to Algebra.
Also see Chapter 3, Applying Equations; Chapter 4, More Applications;
and *Supplement*, Translating Expressions.

33. The line goes through the points (2,0) and (0,- 1). Both points must
    check in the correct equations for line L.

Check (2,0)

$y = - 1$ $x = 2$ $y = x - 1$
$0 = - 1$ $2 = 2$ $0 = 2 - 1$
not true   true $0 = 1$
                                               not true

$y = 2x - 1$ $y = \frac{1}{2}x - 1$
$0 = 2(2) - 1$
$0 = 4 - 1$ $0 = \frac{1}{2}(2) - 1$
not true
                                   $0 = 1 - 1$
                                   $0 = 0$
                                   true

Check (0,- 1) in equations (B) and (E).

$x = 2$ $y = \frac{1}{2}x - 1$
$0 = 2$
not true $- 1 = \frac{1}{2}(0) - 1$
                               $- 1 = 0 - 1$
                               $- 1 = - 1$
                               true

The two points both check only in equation (E).

Answer E

Or, find the slope of the line using the two given points, and then
determine the equation using the slope and the y-intercept.

Reference: *Text*. Chapter 7, Section 7.1, Solutions of Equations in Two Variables; Section 7.2, The Rectangular Coordinate System; Section 7.3, Graphing Linear Equations. Or, see Section 7.4, Slope of a Line.

34. Replace x with 2:

$$P = 10(5)^x$$
$$P = 10(5)^2$$
$$P = 10(5)(5)$$
$$P = 250$$

Answer B

Reference: Text. Chapter 1, Section 1.6, Evaluating Algebraic Expressions.

35.
$$4x - 3 = y$$
$$4x - 3 + 3 = y + 3$$
$$4x = y + 3$$
$$\frac{1}{4} \cdot 4x = \frac{1}{4} \cdot (y + 3)$$
$$x = \frac{y + 3}{4}$$

Answer B

Reference: *Text*. Chapter 3, Section 3.4, Combining the Rules to Solve Equations.

36. Use the Pythagorean Theorem.

$$c^2 = a^2 + b^2$$
$$h^2 = 2^2 + 3^2$$
$$h^2 = 4 + 9$$
$$h^2 = 13$$
$$h = \sqrt{13}$$

Answer E

Reference: *Text*. Chapter 10, Section 10.4, The Pythagorean Theorem.

37. Solve the system of linear equations by adding

$$x - y = 3$$
$$\underline{2x + y = -6}$$
$$3x \quad\ \ = -3$$
$$x \quad\ = -1$$

$$x - y = 3$$
$$-1 - y = 3$$
$$-1 + 1 - y = 3 + 1$$
$$-y = 4$$
$$y = -4$$

Substitute $x = -1$ into either original equation.

Answer A

Reference: *Text*. Chapter 8, Section 8.1, Systems of Linear Equations: Solving by Adding.

38. Let the number of students studying less than 6 hours = x.
The total number of students is 40 + x.
Set up a proportion and solve.

$$\frac{4}{5} = \frac{40}{x + 40}$$
$$4(x + 40) = 5(40)$$
$$4x + 160 = 200$$
$$4x = 40$$
$$x = 10$$

Answer D

Reference: *Text*. Chapter 6, Section 6.9, Ratio and Proportion.

39. Area of a square = s^2
Perimeter of a square = 4s
For fencing, use the perimeter formula.

$$P = 4s$$
$$120 \text{ yds} = 4s$$
$$s = 30 \text{ yds}$$

To find the area, use s = 30 yds in the area formula.

$A = s^2$

$A = (30 \text{ yds})^2$

$A = 900 \text{ yds}^2$

Answer A

Reference: *Text*. Chapter1, Section 1.6, Evaluating Algebraic Equations. There is more practice in the *Supplement*: Evaluating Algebraic Expressions -- Applied Problems. Also see the formulas for perimeter, circumference, area and volume inside the back cover of the text.

40. Let the unknown test score = x

To find the average, add up the four scores. Then divide by 4.

$$\frac{72 + 88 + 70 + x}{4} = 80$$

$$\frac{230 + x}{4} = \frac{80}{1}$$

$$230 + x = 320$$

$$x = 90$$

Answer D

Reference: *Supplement*. Whole Numbers, Finding the Average, Word Problems for Linear Equations With One Unknown.

Practice Skills Exam B

1. Three hundred fifty thousand, four hundred is written:
   (A) 350,004   (B) 350,000,400   (C) 350,000.04
   (D) 350,400   (E) 354,400

2. The average of 53, 42, 65 and 80 is
   (A) 240   (B) 60   (C) 24   (D) 65   (E) 97

3. 5 minutes 12 seconds
   <u>-3 minutes 23 seconds</u>

   (A) 8 minutes 35 seconds   (B) 2 minutes 39 seconds
   (C) 2 minutes 11 seconds   (D) 1 minute 49 seconds
   (E) 2 minutes 35 seconds

4. $4715 \div 23$
   (A) 250   (B) 25   (C) 205   (D) 20.5   (E) 20

5. 418 - 39
   (A) 379   (B) 459   (C) 407   (D) 421   (E) 389

6. Which of the following fractions is the largest?
   (A) $\frac{3}{4}$ (B) $\frac{2}{3}$ (C) $\frac{4}{5}$ (D) $\frac{6}{7}$ (E) $\frac{5}{9}$

7. The school dance committee sells 560 tickets at $5.00 each. Food and entertainment cost $1252.00. There was an additional $347.00 in other expenses. How much profit was made?

   (A) $1548   (B) $1599   (C) $2800   (D) $2453   (E) $1201

8. $\frac{3}{5} + \frac{2}{7} =$
   (A) $\frac{5}{12}$ (B) $\frac{5}{35}$ (C) $\frac{1}{35}$ (D) $\frac{31}{35}$ (E) $\frac{35}{12}$

9. $3\frac{1}{3} - 2\frac{3}{4}$
   (A) $6\frac{1}{12}$ (B) $1\frac{7}{12}$ (C) $1\frac{5}{12}$ (D) $5\frac{5}{12}$ (E) $\frac{7}{12}$

10. $5\frac{2}{3} \div 3\frac{2}{3}$

   (A) $1\frac{6}{11}$ (B) 2   (C) $5\frac{2}{3}$ (D) $20\frac{7}{9}$ (E) $\frac{11}{17}$

11. Which of the following numbers is <u>smallest</u>?
   (A) .8030   (B) .8300   (C) .9   (D) .0099   (E) .08

12. 12.058 + 7 + 3.04 =
   (A) 15.798   (B) 15.168   (C) 15.205   (D) 22.098   (E) 82.098

13. 49.5 - 3.78
   (A) 45.88   (B) 46.28   (C) 46.73   (D) 45.72   (E) 45.28

14. Change $\frac{5}{7}$ to a decimal number rounded to the nearest hundredth.

   (A) .07   (B) .714   (C) .71   (D) 7.14   (E) .700

15. The student bookstore sells 32 T-shirts priced at $4.95 each. What are the total sales?

   (A) $15,840   (B) $1584   (C) $2575   (D) $257.50   (E) $158.40

16. The graph below pictures the book order for each department of a local school. Find the total cost of all book orders.

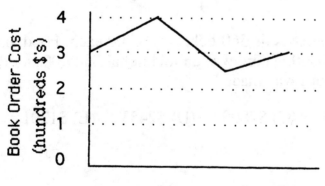

   (A) $165   (B) $1650   (C) $1250   (D) $12.5   (E) $12,500

17. 70% of 180 is
   (A) 140   (B) 126   (C) 120   (D) 240   (E) 261

18. If 20% of a number is 40, what is the number?
    (A) 200   (B) 800   (C) 8   (D) 20   (E) 2000

19. If a \$35 shirt is marked down by 15%, what is its sale price?

    (A) \$20   (B) \$20.75   (C) \$50   (D) \$29.75   (E) \$30.50

20. Find the perimeter of a rectangular garden that is 18 feet long and 12 feet wide.
    (A) 216 feet   (B) 60 feet   (C) 30 feet   (D) 216 square feet
    (E) 6 feet

21. The sum of $7a + 2b$ and $6a - 2b$ is:
    (A) $13a - 4b$ (B) a (C) $13a$ (D) $42a^2 - 4b^2$
    (E) $13a^2$

22. The product of $4x^2y^3z$ and $- 3xy^4z^2$ is:
    (A) $- 12x^2y^{12}z^2$ (B) $- 12x^3y^7z^3$ (C) $- 7x^2y^7z^2$ (D) $12x^2y^{12}z^2$
    (E) $7x^3y^7z^3$

23. Simplify: $\dfrac{8x^2 + 12x}{- 2x}$
    (A) $4x - 6$ (B) $4x - 6x$ (C) $- 4x^2 - 10$ (D) $- 4x - 6$ (E) $4x + 6$

24. Simplify: $3a^2 - 5a(a - 2)$
    (A) $- 2a^2 + 10a$ (B) $- 2a^2 + a - 2$ (C) $- 8a^2 + 10a$ (D) $- 2a^2 - 10a$
    (E) $2a^2 - 10a$

25. Add $4y^2 - 3y + 7$ and $y^2 - 6$
    (A) $5y^2 - 9y + 7$ (B) $5y^2 - 3y + 1$ (C) $8y^2 + 1$
    (D) $5y^2 - 3y - 13$ (E) $4y^2 - 2y + 1$

26. $(3x^4y^3)^2$
    (A) $6x^6y^5$ (B) $9x^6y^5$ (C) $9x^7y^7$ (D) $28x^8y^6$
    (E) $9x^8y^6$

27. Factor: $8a^3 - 12a^2$
    (A) $- 4a$ (B) $4a^3(2 - 3a)$ (C) $4(2a - 3)$ (D) $12a(4a^2 - a)$
    (E) $4a^2(2a - 3)$

28. $5 - 3(-3)^2 + 1$
   (A) - 21   (B) 21   (C) 19   (D) 17   (E) - 19

29. If $3x + 2 = 5x - 6$, then x =
   (A) 8   (B) 4   (C) 16   (D) - 4   (E) - 16

30. If $\dfrac{2}{-4} = \dfrac{7}{x}$, then x =
   (A) 14   (B) - 8   (C) - 14   (D) 9   (E) - 9

31. Which of the following points lies on the graph of $3x + y = 7$?
   (A) (1,2)   (B) (3,1)   (C) (3,7)   (D) (1,3)   (E) (2,1)

32. Suppose wallets cost \$12 and keychains cost \$8. What is the cost of x wallets and y keychains?

   (A) 12x + 8y dollars   (B) 20xy dollars   (C) 96xy dollars
   (D) 8x + 12y dollars   (E) 20x + 20y dollars

33. An equation for the line L on the right is:

   (A) 3x - 2y = - 6
   (B) 2x - 3y = - 6
   (C) x - y = 1
   (D) x = - 2
   (E) y = 3

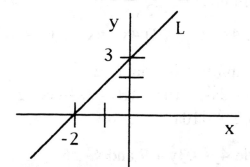

34. If $x = 2$ and $y = - 4$, find the value of $x^3 - 3xy$.
   (A) 30   (B) - 16   (C) 32   (D) - 30   (E) - 18

35. If $a + 3b = 7$, then b =
   (A) - 3a + 7   (B) 7 - 3a   (C) $\dfrac{7a}{3}$ (D) $\dfrac{7 - a}{3}$ (E) 4 - a

36. In the right triangle shown here, find x.

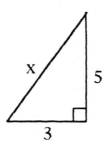

(A) 8   (B) 4   (C) $\sqrt{34}$ (D) 17   (E) 6

37. If $3A + 2B = 0$ and $-3A + B = -9$, then
   (A) A = 2 and B = - 3   (B) A = 3 and B = - 2
   (C) A = 0 and B = - 2   (D) A = - 3 and B = 0
   (E) A = - 3 and B = 2

38. Three out of every 7 applicants were seleted for the Math Fair. How many applicants were there if there were 54 entries in the competition?

   (A) 1134   (B) 378   (C) 126   (D) 87   (E) 113

39. If $y = 3x^2z$, find y when $x = -2$ and $z = 4$

   (A) - 48   (B) 11   (C) - 11   (D) 132   (E) 48

40. It costs the organizers of a Lafayette High School reunion $6 per person to cater the affair. Additionally, there are $224 in other costs. If there is a $10 charge per person to attend the reunion, how many people must attend before they break even?

   (A) 56   (B) 65   (C) 23   (D) 900   (E) 50

1. Three hundred fifty thousand four hundred is written 350,400.
   Answer: D
   Reference: *Supplement.* Whole numbers, Writing a Number.

2. The average of 53, 42, 65, and 80 is $\dfrac{53 + 42 + 65 + 80}{4} = \dfrac{240}{4} = 60$

   Answer B
   Reference: *Supplement.* Whole numbers, Averages.

3. 5 minutes 12 seconds = 4 minutes 72 seconds
   <u>-3 minutes 23 seconds</u> = <u>3 minutes 23 seconds</u>
                          1 minute 49 seconds

   Answer D
   Reference: *Supplement.* Measurement.

4. $$\begin{array}{r} 205 \\ 23\overline{)4715} \\ \underline{-46} \\ 115 \\ \underline{-115} \end{array}$$

   Answer C
   Reference: *Supplement.* Whole numbers, Division.

5. $$\begin{array}{r} 418 \\ \underline{-\ 39} \\ 379 \end{array}$$

   Answer A
   Reference: *Supplement.* Whole numbers, Subtraction.

6. $\frac{3}{4} = .75$ $\frac{2}{3} \approx .67$ $\frac{4}{5} = .80$ $\frac{6}{7} \approx .86$ $\frac{5}{9} \approx .56$

$$4\overline{)3.00} \quad \begin{array}{r} .75 \\ -28 \\ \hline 20 \\ -20 \\ \hline \end{array}$$

$$3\overline{)2.00} \quad \begin{array}{r} .66 \\ -18 \\ \hline 20 \\ -18 \\ \hline 2 \end{array}$$

$$5\overline{)4.00} \quad \begin{array}{r} .80 \\ -40 \\ \hline 00 \end{array}$$

$$7\overline{)6.00} \quad \begin{array}{r} .85 \\ -56 \\ \hline 40 \\ -35 \\ \hline 5 \end{array}$$

$$9\overline{)5.00} \quad \begin{array}{r} .55 \\ -45 \\ \hline 50 \\ -45 \\ \hline 5 \end{array}$$

Answer: D

Reference: *Text.*. Appendix 1. Equivalent fractions; Finding the Least Common Denominator.
Or, change the fractions to decimal numbers and then compare. See *Supplement.*, Converting a fraction to a decimal number, Comparing decimal numbers.

7. Profit = Income - Expenses

The income from selling the tickets was $2800.
(560 x $5 = $2800)

The expenses are $1252 + $347 = $1599.

Profit = $2800 - $1599 = $1201.

Answer E
Reference: *Supplement.* Whole numbers and Word Problems.

8. $\frac{3}{5} + \frac{2}{7}$

The LCD for 5 and 7 is 35.

$$\frac{3}{5} = \frac{(7)3}{(7)5} = \frac{21}{35} \qquad \frac{2}{7} = \frac{(5)2}{(5)7} = \frac{10}{35}$$

$$\frac{21}{35} + \frac{10}{35} = \frac{31}{35}$$

Answer D
Reference: *Text* . Appendix 1 Adding Unlike Fractions.

9.

$$3\frac{1}{3} = 3\frac{4}{12} = 2\frac{16}{12}$$

$$-2\frac{3}{4} = 2\frac{9}{12} = 2\frac{9}{12}$$

$$\frac{7}{12}$$

Answer E

Reference: *Text*. Appendix 1 Adding or Subtracting Mixed Numbers.

10. $5\frac{2}{3} \div 3\frac{2}{3} = \frac{17}{3} \div \frac{11}{3}$

$$= \frac{17}{3} \times \frac{3}{11}$$

$$= \frac{17 \times \overset{1}{\cancel{3}}}{\underset{1}{\cancel{3}} \times 11}$$

$$= \frac{17}{11}$$

$$= 1\frac{6}{11}$$

Answer A

Reference: *Text* . Appendix 1 Multiplying or Dividing Mixed Numbers.

11. .8030 = .8030
.8300 = .8300
.9   = .9000
.0099 = .0099
.08   = .0800

The smallest number is .0099

Answer D

Reference: *Supplement*. Comparing Decimal Numbers.

12. 12.058
      7.000
    + 3.040
     22.098

Answer D

Reference: *Supplement.* Adding Decimal Numbers.

13. 49.50
    - 3.78
     45.72

Answer D

Reference: *Supplement.* Subtracting Decimal Numbers.

14. $\dfrac{5}{7} = 5 \div 7$

$$
\begin{array}{r}
.714... \\
7\overline{)5.000} \\
4\,9 \\
\hline
10 \\
-7 \\
\hline
30 \\
-28 \\
\hline
2
\end{array}
$$

Round to the nearest hundredth .714... becomes .71

Answer C

Reference: *Supplement.* Changing a Fraction to a Decimal Number

15. Number of shirts x price for each shirt = 32 x $4.95 = $158.40
    Answer E

Reference: *Supplement.* Multiplying Decimal Numbers.

16.   English   = $300

         Math   = $400

         Science   = $250

         Language   = $300

                      $1250

Answer C

Reference: *Supplement*. Graphs.

17. 70% of 180 is

.70 x 180 = 126.00 = 126

Answer B

Reference: *Supplement*. Per Cents.

18. 20% of a number is 40

$.20 \times N = 40$

$$N = \frac{40}{.20}$$

OR

$$\frac{20}{100} = \frac{40}{N}$$

$20 \times N = 100 \times 40$

$20 \times N = 4000$

$$N = \frac{4000}{20}$$

$N = 200$

$N = 200$

Answer A

Reference: *Supplement*. Per Cents.

19. Find 15% of $35. Then subtract it from $35.

15% of $35 = .15 x $35

= $5.25

$35 - $5.25 = $29.75

Answer D

Reference: *Supplement*. Per Cents.

20. The perimeter of a rectangle = 2 x length + 2 x width

$$= 2 \text{ x } 18 \text{ feet} + 2 \text{ x } 12 \text{ feet}$$
$$= 36 \text{ feet} + 24 \text{ feet}$$
$$= 60 \text{ feet}$$

Answer B

Reference: *Text.* Chapter 1, Section 1.6, Evaluating Algebraic Expressions. Also see *Supplement.* Evaluating Algebraic Expressions - - Applied Problems.

21. $(7a + 2b) + (6a - 2b) = 7a + 2b + 6a - 2b$
$$= 13a$$

Answer C

Reference: *Text.* Chapter 4, Section 4.2, Adding and Subtracting Polynomials.

22. $(4x^2 y^3 z)(- 3xy^4 z^2) = - 12x^3 y^7 z^3$

Answer B

Reference: *Text.* Chapter 1, Section 1.5, Multiplying Expressions. Chapter 4, Multiplying Monomials.

23. $\dfrac{8x^2 + 12x}{-2x} = \dfrac{8x^2}{-2x} + \dfrac{12x}{-2x}$
$$= - 4x - 6$$

Answer D

Reference: Text. Chapter 4, Section 4.5, Dividing Polynomials.

24. $3a^2 - 5a(a - 2) = 3a^2 - 5a^2 + 10a$
$$= - 2a^2 + 10a$$

Answer A

Reference: *Text.* Chapter 4, Section 4.3, Multiplying Polynomials.

25. $(4y^2 - 3y + 7) + (y^2 - 6) = 4y^2 - 3y + 7 + y^2 - 6$
$$= 5y^2 - 3y + 1$$

Answer B

Reference: *Text*. Chapter 4, Section 4.2, Adding and Subtracting Polynomials.

26. $(3x^4y^3)^2 = (3x^4y^3)(3x^4y^3)$ or $(3)^2(x^4)^2(y^3)^2$
$= 9x^8y^6$

Answer E

Reference: *Text*. Chapter 9, Section 9.1, Extending the Properties of Exponents.

27. $8a^3 - 12a^2$
The GCF is $4a^2$
$4a^2(2a - 3)$

Answer E

Reference: *Text*. Chapter 5, Factoring a monomial from a polynomial.

28. $5 - 3(-3)^2 + 1$
$5 - 3(+9) + 1$
$5 - 27 + 1$
-21

Answer A

Reference: *Text*. Chapter 1, Section 1.6, Evaluating Algebraic Expressions. Also see Chapter 2, Section 2.4, Multiplying Signed Numbers.

29.
$$3x + 2 = 5x - 6$$
$$3x - 5x = -2 - 6$$
$$\frac{-2x}{-2} = \frac{-8}{-2}$$
$$x = +4$$

Answer B

Reference: *Text*. Chapter 3, Section 3.4, Combining Rules to Solve Equations.

30.
$$\frac{2}{-4} = \frac{7}{x}$$
$$\frac{2x}{2} = \frac{-28}{2} \text{ by cross-multiplication}$$
$$x = -14$$

Answer C

Reference: *Text*. Chapter 6, Section 6.7, Equations Involving Fractions.

31. Check to see which ordered pair (x,y) satisfies the equation.

(1,2)	(3,1)	(3,7)
$3x + y = 7$	$3x + y = 7$	$3x + y = 7$
$3(1) + 2 = 7$	$3(3) + 1 = 7$	$3(3) + 7 = 7$
$3 + 2 = 7$	$9 + 1 = 7$	$9 + 7 = 7$
$5 = 7$	$10 = 7$	$16 = 7$
Not true	Not true	Not true

(1,3)

$$3x + y = 7$$
$$3(1) + 3 = 7$$
$$3 + 3 = 7$$
$$6 = 7$$

Not true

(2,1)

$$3x + y = 7$$
$$3(2) + 1 = 7$$
$$6 + 1 = 7$$
$$7 = 7$$

True

Answer E

Reference: *Text* . Chapter 7, Sections 7.1, Solutions of Equations in Two Variables.

32. x wallets for $12 each is $12x.
y keychains for $8 each is $8y.
The total of $12x and $8y is 12x + 8y dollars.

Answer A

Reference: *Text.* Chapter 1, From Arithmetic to Algebra. Also see *Supplement*, Translating Expressions.

33. The line goes through the points (- 2,0) and (0,3). Both points must check in the correct equation for line L.

Check (- 2,0)

$$3x - 2y = -6$$
$$3(-2) - 2(0) = -6$$
$$-6 - 0 = -6$$
$$-6 = -6$$

True

$$2x - 3y = -6$$
$$2(-2) - 3(0) = -6$$
$$-4 - 0 = -6$$
$$-4 = -6$$

Not true

$$x - y = 1$$
$$-2 - 0 = 1$$
$$-2 = 1$$

Not true

$$x = -2$$
$$-2 = -2$$
True

$$y = 3$$
$$0 = 3$$
Not true

Check (0,3) in equations (A) and (D).

$$3x - 2y = -6$$
$$3(0) - 2(3) = -6$$
$$0 - 6 = -6$$
$$-6 = -6$$
True

$$x = -2$$
$$0 = -2$$
Not true

The two points both check only in equation (A).

Or, find the slope of the line using the two given points, and then determine the equation using the slope and the y-intercept.

Answer A

Reference: *Text*. Chapter 7, Section 7.1, Solutions of Equations in Two Variables; Section 7.2, The Rectangular Coordinate System; Section 7.3, Graphing Linear Equations. Or, see Section 7.4, Slope of a Line.

34. Replace x with 2 and y with - 4:

$$x^3 - 3xy$$
$$2^3 - 3(2)(-4)$$
$$8 + 24$$
$$32$$

Answer C

Reference: Text. Chapter 1, Section 1.6, Evaluating Algebraic Expressions.

35. $a + 3b = 7$
$$\frac{3b}{3} = \frac{7 - a}{3}$$
$$b = \frac{7 - a}{3}$$

Answer D

Reference: *Text*. Chapter 3, Section 3.4, Combining the Rules to Solve Equations.

36. Use the Pythagorean Theorem.

$$c^2 = a^2 + b^2$$
$$x^2 = 3^2 + 5^2$$
$$x^2 = 9 + 25$$
$$x^2 = 34$$
$$x = \sqrt{34}$$

Answer C

Reference: *Text*. Chapter 10, Section 10.4, The Pythagorean Theorem.

37. Solve the system of linear equations by adding

$$3A + 2B = 0$$
$$-3A + B = -9$$
$$\frac{3B}{3} = \frac{-9}{3}$$
$$B = -3$$

$$-3A + B = -9$$
$$-3A + (-3) = -9$$
$$-3A - 3 = -9$$
$$-3A - 3 + 3 = -9 + 3$$
$$\frac{-3A}{-3} = \frac{-6}{-3}$$
$$A = 2$$

Substitute B = -3 into either original equation.

Answer A

Reference: *Text*. Chapter 8, Section 8.1, Systems of Linear Equations: Solving by Adding.

38. Let the number of applicants = x.
    Set up a proportion and solve.

$$\frac{\text{Number selected}}{\text{Number of applicants}}$$

$$\frac{3}{7} = \frac{54}{x}$$

$$3(x) = 7(54)$$

$$\frac{3x}{3} = \frac{378}{3}$$

$$x = 126$$

Answer C

Reference: *Text*. Chapter 6, Section 6.9, Ratio and Proportion.

39. Replace x with - 2 and z with 4.

$$y = 3x^2z$$

$$y = 3(-2)^2(4)$$

$$y = 3(4)(4)$$

$$y = 48$$

Answer E

Reference: *Text*. Chapter1, Section 1.6, Evaluating Algebraic Expressions. There is more practice in the *Supplement*: Evaluating Algebraic Expressions -- Applied Problems. Also see the formulas for perimeter, circumference, area and volume inside the back cover of the text.

40. Since the cost is $6 per person and the charge is $10 per person, a $4 profit is made on each person attending the reunion (not counting the additional costs). We must divide the additional costs of $224 by $4 to determine how many people must attend before they break even.

```
      56
   4)224
   -20
     24
    -24
```

56 people must attend before they break even.

Answer A

Reference: *Supplement*. Whole Numbers, Finding the Average, Word Problems for Linear Equations With One Unknown.

Practice Skills Exam C

1. Twelve million, twelve thousand is written:
   (A) 12,000,000,12,000   (B) 12,000,000,012,000   (C) 12,012,000
   (D) 12,000,000.012   (E) 12,000,000.12000

2. The average of 15, 20, 0 and 25 is
   (A) 20   (B) 60   (C) 15   (D) 55   (E) 0

3. 5 weeks 2 days
   -3 weeks 3 days

   (A) 1week 6 days   (B) 2 weeks 6 days   (C) 2 weeks 1 day
   (D) 2 weeks 9 days   (E) 1 week 9 days

4. 8154 ÷ 27
   (A) 3.2   (B) 320   (C) 3020   (D) 32   (E) 302

5. 607 - 99
   (A) 698   (B) 502   (C) 512   (D) 508   (E) 607.99

6. Which of the following fractions is the largest?
   (A) $\frac{5}{6}$ (B) $\frac{7}{8}$ (C) $\frac{7}{10}$ (D) $\frac{7}{12}$ (E) $\frac{5}{8}$

7. The seller in the ticket booth sold 300 tickets for the 1:00 PM show. 200 adult tickets at $7.00 each were sold. The rest of the tickets sold were children's tickets at $5.00 each. The movie cost $1200 to show. How much profit was made?

   (A) $1400   (B) $300   (C) $500   (D) $700   (E) $1900

8. $\frac{3}{7}+\frac{2}{3}=$
   (A) $\frac{5}{10}$ (B) $\frac{1}{2}$ (C) $\frac{6}{21}$ (D) $\frac{23}{21}$ (E) $\frac{5}{21}$

9. $7\frac{1}{3}-6\frac{2}{3}$
   (A) $1\frac{1}{3}$ (B) $\frac{2}{3}$ (C) $1\frac{9}{3}$ (D) $\frac{9}{3}$ (E) $1\frac{2}{3}$

10. $8\frac{1}{10} \div 30$

   (A) $\frac{27}{100}$ (B) 243   (C) $2\frac{7}{10}$ (D) $\frac{8}{300}$ (E) $8\frac{1}{300}$

11. Which of the following numbers is <u>smallest</u>?
    (A) .677   (B) .0766   (C) .77   (D) .0066   (E) .06

12. 3.04 + 5 + 0.067 =
    (A) 8.107   (B) 3.607   (C) 3.112   (D) 0.376   (E) .00376

13. 17.8 - 4.75
    (A) 11.15   (B) 13.15   (C) 13.05   (D) 12.15   (E) 12.05

14. Change $\frac{7}{9}$ to a decimal number rounded to the nearest hundredth.

    (A) 1.29   (B) .778   (C) .78   (D) 7.9   (E) 1.28

15. A three-pound bag of apples is on sale for $1.05. How much will seven bags cost?
    (A) $10.50   (B) $7.35   (C) $2.45   (D) $3.15   (E) $7.75

16. The graph below pictures the amount of money raised for a food program in one day by each class. What is the total amount raised?

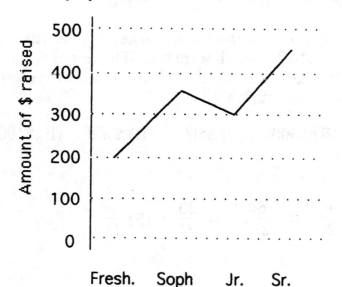

    (A) $500   (B) $650   (C) $1250   (D) $1300   (E) $450

17. 45% of 50 is

(A) 225   (B) 2.25   (C) 22.5   (D) 0.225   (E) 2250

18. If a $225 suit is reduced by 40% at a big sale, what is its sale price?

(A) $90   (B) $185   (C) $135   (D) $216   (E) $200

19. If 40% of a number is 36, what is the number?

(A) 144   (B) 14.4   (C) 1.44   (D) 900   (E) 90

20. A rectangular table top is 5 feet long and 3 feet wide. What is the area of the table top?

(A) 15 feet   (B) 16 feet   (C) 15 square feet   (D) 16 square feet
(E) 8 feet

21. The sum of $4x + 3y$ and $-5x - 7y$ is:

(A) $x - 4y$ (B) $-x + 10y$ (C) $-9x - 10y$ (D) $x - 10y$
(E) $-x - 4y$

22. The product of $-3a^3b^4$ and $-5ab^2c^2$ is:

(A) $-15a^3b^8c^2$ (B) $-15a^4b^8c^2$ (C) $-15a^4b^6c^2$ (D) $15a^3b^6c^2$
(E) $15a^3b^8c^2$

23. Simplify: $\dfrac{9x^6 + 3x^2}{-3x^2}$

(A) $-3x^4 - 1$ (B) $-3x^3 - 1$ (C) $-3x^4$ (D) $-4x^4$ (E) $-3x^3$

24. Simplify: $-4x^3 - 3x(x^2 + x)$

(A) $-7x^3 - 3x^2$ (B) $-10x$ (C) $7x^3 - 3x^2$ (D) $-10x^5$
(E) $-4x^3 - 3x^4$

25. Add $3y^2 - 4y + 6$ and $y^2 - 7$

(A) $4y^2 - 4y - 13$ (B) $8y^2 - 1$ (C) $3y^2 - 4y - 1$
(D) $3y^2 - 4y - 13$ (E) $4y^2 - 4y - 1$

26. $(-2x^3y^4)^3$

(A) $-6x^6y^7$ (B) $8x^6y^7$ (C) $8x^9y^{12}$ (D) $-8x^9y^{12}$
(E) $-8x^{21}y^{21}$

27. Factor: $10b^4 - 25b^2$
   (A) $5b^2$ (B) $- 15b^2$ (C) $5b(2b^4 - 5b^2)$ (D) $(5b^2 + 5b)(2b^2 - 5b)$
   (E) $5b^2(2b^2 - 5)$

28. $7 - 3(- 2)^3 - 4$
   (A) $- 36$ (B) $- 28$ (C) 35 (D) 27 (E) $- 16$

29. If $5x - 2 = 7x - 10$, then $x =$
   (A) 3 (B) $- 3$ (C) 2 (D) $- 4$ (E) 4

30. If $\dfrac{4}{-3} = \dfrac{a}{-6}$, then $a =$
   (A) $- 2$ (B) $- 8$ (C) 6 (D) 8 (E) 4

31. Which of the following points lies on the graph of $4x - y = 3$?
   (A) $(2,5)$ (B) $(1, - 2)$ (C) $(- 1, - 2)$ (D) $(0,3)$ (E) $(2,- 5)$

32. Suppose hats cost $8 and gloves cost $6. What is the cost of h hats and g gloves?

   (A) 4hg dollars   (B) 14hg dollars   (C) 14h + 14g dollars
   (D) 8h + 6g dollars   (E) 48h + 48g dollars

33. An equation for the line L on
   the right is:

   (A) $x = - 2$
   (B) $y = 2$
   (C) $y = x + 2$
   (D) $x = y + 2$
   (E) $x + y = 2$

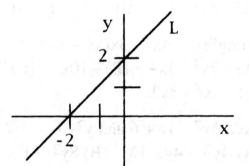

34. If $a = 3$ and $b = - 2$, find the value of $b^3 - 2a^2b$.
   (A) $- 44$ (B) $- 2$ (C) 28 (D) $- 28$ (E) 24

35. If $- 5x + 2y = - 6$, then $y =$
   (A) $5x - 3y$ (B) $\dfrac{5x - 6}{2}$ (C) $\dfrac{- 5x - 6}{2}$ (D) $- 5x - 3$ (E) $\dfrac{- x}{2}$

36. In the right triangle shown here, find x.

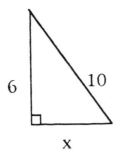

(A) $\sqrt{136}$ (B) 4   (C) $\sqrt{8}$ (D) 16   (E) 8

37. If $2x - 4y = 4$ and $-3x + 4y = 16$, then
   (A) $x = 4$ and $y = 1$ (B) $x = 4$ and $y = -1$
   (C) $x = 2$ and $y = 3$ (D) $x = 1$ and $y = 4$
   (E) $x = -1$ and $y = -4$

38. If two out of every five college students at School A exercise daily, how many college students are there at School A, if 1,036 students exercise daily?

   (A) 207   (B) 10,360   (C) 8,465   (D) 2,590   (E) 5,180

39. If $a = 4bc^3$, find a when $b = -3$ and $c = -2$

   (A) 96   (B) -48   (C) 24   (D) 72   (E) -72

40. John needs a 90 average in Mathematics to be eligible for the Honor Society. He receives a 65, 100, 90 and 95 on his first four exams. What is the lowest grade he can score on the last exam to be eligible for the Honor Society?

   (A) 90   (B) 95   (C) 92   (D) 85   (E) 100

Solutions for the Practice Skills Exam C with References

1. Twelve million, twelve thousand is written 12,012,000.
   Answer: C
   Reference: *Supplement.* Whole numbers, Writing a Number.

2. The average of 15, 20, 0 and 25 is $\dfrac{15 + 20 + 0 + 25}{4} = \dfrac{60}{4} = 15$

   Answer C
   Reference: *Supplement.* Whole numbers, Averages.

3. 5 weeks 2 days = 4 weeks 9 days
   <u>-3 weeks 3 days</u> = <u>3 weeks 3 days</u>
                  1 week   6 days

   Answer A
   Reference: *Supplement.* Measurement.

4.
$$
\begin{array}{r}
302 \\
27\overline{)8154} \\
\underline{-81} \\
054 \\
\underline{-\,54} \\
\end{array}
$$

   Answer E
   Reference: *Supplement.* Whole numbers, Division.

5.
$$
\begin{array}{r}
607 \\
\underline{-\,99} \\
508 \\
\end{array}
$$

   Answer D
   Reference: *Supplement.* Whole numbers, Subtraction.

6. $\frac{5}{6} \approx .83$ $\frac{7}{8} = .875$ $\frac{7}{10} = .7$ $\frac{7}{12} \approx .58$ $\frac{5}{8} = .625$

$$
\begin{array}{r}
.833 \\
6\overline{)5.000} \\
-48 \\
\hline
20 \\
-18 \\
\hline
20 \\
-18 \\
\end{array}
\qquad
\begin{array}{r}
.875 \\
8\overline{)7.000} \\
-64 \\
\hline
60 \\
-56 \\
\hline
40 \\
-40 \\
\end{array}
\qquad
\begin{array}{r}
.7 \\
10\overline{)7.0} \\
-70 \\
\hline
\end{array}
\qquad
\begin{array}{r}
.583 \\
12\overline{)7.000} \\
-60 \\
\hline
100 \\
-96 \\
\hline
40 \\
-36 \\
\end{array}
\qquad
\begin{array}{r}
.625 \\
8\overline{)5.000} \\
-48 \\
\hline
20 \\
-16 \\
\hline
40 \\
-40 \\
\end{array}
$$

Answer: B

Reference: *Text..* Appendix 1. Equivalent fractions; Finding the Least Common Denominator.
Or, change the fractions to decimal numbers and then compare. See *Supplement.*, Converting a fraction to a decimal number, Comparing decimal numbers.

7. Profit = Income - Expenses

The income from selling the tickets was $1900.
Adult tickets: 200 x $7 = $1400
Children's tickets: 100 x $5 = $500
Total sales: $1400 + $500 = $1900

The expenses are $1200.

Profit = $1900 - $1200 = $700.

Answer D
Reference: *Supplement.* Whole numbers and Word Problems.

8. $\frac{3}{7} + \frac{2}{3}$

The LCD for 7 and 3 is 21.
$$\frac{3}{7} = \frac{(3)3}{(3)7} = \frac{9}{21} \qquad \frac{2}{3} = \frac{(7)2}{(7)3} = \frac{14}{21}$$
$$\frac{9}{21} + \frac{14}{21} = \frac{23}{21}$$
Answer D
Reference: *Text* . Appendix 1 Adding Unlike Fractions.

9.

$$7\frac{1}{3} = 6\frac{4}{3}$$

$$-6\frac{2}{3} = 6\frac{2}{3}$$

$$\frac{2}{3}$$

Answer B

Reference: *Text.* Appendix 1 Adding or Subtracting Mixed Numbers.

10. $8\dfrac{1}{10} \div 30 = \dfrac{81}{10} \div \dfrac{30}{1}$

$$= \frac{81}{10} \times \frac{1}{30}$$

$$= \frac{\overset{27}{\cancel{81}} \times 1}{10 \times \underset{10}{\cancel{30}}}$$

$$= \frac{27}{100}$$

Answer A

Reference: *Text* . Appendix 1 Multiplying or Dividing Mixed Numbers.

11. $.677 = .6770$

$.0766 = .0766$

$.77 = .7700$

$.0066 = .0066$

$.06 = .0600$

The smallest number is .0066

Answer D

Reference: *Supplement.* Comparing Decimal Numbers.

12.   3.040
      5.000
    + 0.067
      8.107

Answer A

Reference: *Supplement.* Adding Decimal Numbers.

13. 17.80
    - 4.75
     13.05

Answer C

Reference: *Supplement.* Subtracting Decimal Numbers.

14. $\frac{7}{9} = 7 \div 9$

$$= 9\overline{)7.000} \quad .777...$$

$$\begin{array}{r} .777... \\ 9\overline{)7.000} \\ \underline{6\ 3} \\ 70 \\ \underline{-63} \\ 70 \\ \underline{-63} \\ 7 \end{array}$$

Round to the nearest hundredth .777... becomes .78

Answer C

Reference: *Supplement.* Changing a Fraction to a Decimal Number

15. Number of bags x price for each bag = 7 x $1.05 = $7.35
    Answer B
    Reference: *Supplement* . Multiplying Decimal Numbers.

16.　Fresh.　　= $200

　　　Soph　　= $350

　　　Jr.　　 = $300

　　　Sr.　　 = $450 (underlined)

　　　　　　　$1300

Answer D
Reference: *Supplement*. Graphs.

17. 45% of 50 is
.45 x 50 = 22.50 = 22.5

Answer C

Reference: *Supplement*. Per Cents.

18. Find 40% of $225. Then subtract it from $225.
40% of $225 = .40 x $225
　　　　　　 = $90
$225 - $90　 = $135

Answer C
Reference: *Supplement*. Per Cents.

19. 40% of a number is 36

.40 × N = 36

$$N = \frac{36}{.40}$$

$$N = 90$$

OR

$$\frac{40}{100} = \frac{36}{N}$$

40 × N = 100 × 36

40 × N = 3600

$$N = \frac{3600}{40}$$

N = 90

Answer E
Reference: *Supplement*. Per Cents.

20. The areas of a rectangle = length x width

           = 5 feet x 3 feet

           = 15 square feet

Answer C

Reference: *Text.* Chapter 1, Section 1.6, Evaluating Algebraic Expressions. Also see *Supplement.* Evaluating Algebraic Expressions - - Applied Problems.

21. $(4x + 3y) + (- 5x - 7y) = 4x + 3y - 5x - 7y$

             $= - x - 4y$

Answer E

Reference: *Text.* Chapter 4, Section 4.2, Adding and Subtracting Polynomials.

22. $(- 3a^3b^4)(- 5ab^2c^2) = + 15a^3b^6c^2$

Answer D

Reference: *Text.* Chapter 1, Section 1.5, Multiplying Expressions. Chapter 4, Multiplying Monomials.

23. $\dfrac{9x^6 + 3x^2}{- 3x^2} = \dfrac{9x^6}{- 3x^2} - \dfrac{3x^2}{- 3x^2}$

        $= - 3x^4 - 1$

Answer A

Reference: Text. Chapter 4, Section 4.5, Dividing Polynomials.

24. $- 4x^3 - 3x(x^2 + x) = - 4x^3 - 3x^3 - 3x^2$

           $= - 7x^3 - 3x^2$

Answer A

Reference: *Text.* Chapter 4, Section 4.3, Multiplying Polynomials.

25. $(3y^2 - 4y + 6) + (y^2 - 7) = 3y^2 - 4y + 6 + y^2 - 7$

             $= 4y^2 - 4y - 1$

Answer E

Reference: *Text.* Chapter 4, Section 4.2, Adding and Subtracting Polynomials.

26. $(-2x^3y^4)^3 = (-2x^3y^4)(-2x^3y^4)(-2x^3y^4)$
$\qquad\qquad = -8x^9y^{12}$

Or

$\quad(-2x^3y^4)^3 = (-2)^3(x^3)^3(y^4)^3$
$\qquad\qquad = -8x^9y^{12}$

Answer D

Reference: *Text*. Chapter 9, Section 9.1, Extending the Properties of Exponents.

27. $10b^4 - 25b^2$
The GCF is $5b^2$
$5b^2(2b^2 - 5)$

Answer E

Reference: *Text*. Chapter 5, Factoring a monomial from a polynomial.

28. $7 - 3(-2)^3 - 4$
$7 - 3(-8) - 4$
$7 + 24 - 4$
27

Answer D

Reference: *Text*. Chapter 1, Section 1.6, Evaluating Algebraic Expressions. Also see Chapter 2, Section 2.4, Multiplying Signed Numbers.

29. $\quad 5x - 2 = 7x - 10$
$\quad -2 + 10 = 7x - 5x$
$$\frac{8}{2} = \frac{2x}{2}$$
$\qquad 4 = x$

Answer E
Reference: *Text*. Chapter 3, Section 3.4, Combining Rules to Solve Equations.

30. $\dfrac{4}{-3} = \dfrac{a}{-6}$

$\dfrac{-3a}{-3} = \dfrac{-24}{-3}$ by cross-multiplication

$a = 8$

Answer D

Reference: *Text.* Chapter 6, Section 6.7, Equations Involving Fractions.

31. Check to see which ordered pair (x,y) satisfies the equation.

(2,5)
$4x - y = 3$
$4(2) - 5 = 3$
$8 - 5 = 3$
$3 = 3$
True

(1,- 2)
$4x - y = 3$
$4(1) - (-2) = 3$
$4 + 2 = 3$
$6 = 3$
Not true

(- 1, - 2)
$4x - y = 3$
$4(-1) - (-2) = 3$
$-4 + 2 = 3$
$-2 = 3$
Not true

(0,3)
$4x - y = 3$
$4(0) - 3 = 3$
$0 - 3 = 3$
$-3 = 3$
Not true

(2,- 5)
$4x - y = 3$
$4(2) - (-5) = 3$
$8 + 5 = 3$
$13 = 3$
Not true

Answer A

Reference: *Text* . Chapter 7, Sections 7.1, Solutions of Equations in Two Variables.

32. h hats for $8 each is $8h.
g gloves for $6 each is $6g.
The total of $8h and $6g is 8h + 6g dollars.

Answer D

Reference: *Text.* Chapter 1, From Arithmetic to Algebra. Also see *Supplement*, Translating Expressions.

33. The line goes through the points (- 2,0) and (0,2). Both points must check in the correct equation for line L.

Check (- 2,0)

$x = -2$	$y = 2$	$y = x + 2$
$-2 = -2$	$0 = 2$	$0 = -2 + 2$
True	Not true	$0 = 0$
		True

$x = y + 2$
$-2 = 0 + 2$
$-2 = 2$
Not true

$x + y = 2$
$-2 + 0 = 2$
$-2 = 2$
Not true

Check (0,2) in equations (A) and (C).

$x = -2$
$0 = -2$
Not true

$y = x + 2$
$2 = 0 + 2$
$2 = 2$
True

The two points both check only in equation (C).

Or, find the slope of the line using the two given points, and then determine the equation using the slope and the y-intercept.

Answer C

Reference: *Text*. Chapter 7, Section 7.1, Solutions of Equations in Two Variables; Section 7.2, The Rectangular Coordinate System; Section 7.3, Graphing Linear Equations. Or, see Section 7.4, Slope of a Line.

34. Replace a with - 3 and b with - 2:

$b^3 - 2a^2b$
$(-2)^3 - 2(-3)^2(-2)$
$-8 - 2(9)(-2)$
$-8 + 36$
28

Answer C

Reference: Text. Chapter 1, Section 1.6, Evaluating Algebraic Expressions.

35. $-5x + 2y = -6$

$$\frac{2y}{2} = \frac{5x - 6}{2}$$

$$y = \frac{5x - 6}{2}$$

Answer B

Reference: *Text*. Chapter 3, Section 3.4, Combining the Rules to Solve Equations.

36. Use the Pythagorean Theorem.

$$c^2 = a^2 + b^2$$
$$10^2 = 6^2 + x^2$$
$$100 = 36 + x^2$$
$$64 = x^2$$
$$8 = x$$

Answer E

Reference: *Text*. Chapter 10, Section 10.4, The Pythagorean Theorem.

37. Solve the system of linear equations by adding

$$2x - 4y = 4$$
$$\underline{3x + 4y = 16}$$
$$\frac{5x}{5} = \frac{20}{5}$$
$$x = 4$$

$$2x - 4y = 4$$
$$2(4) - 4y = 4$$
$$8 - 4y = 4$$
$$\frac{-4y}{-4} = \frac{-4}{-4}$$
$$y = 1$$

Substitute x = 4 into either original equation.

Answer A

Reference: *Text.* Chapter 8, Section 8.1, Systems of Linear Equations: Solving by Adding.

38. Let the number of students who exercise daily = x.
Set up a proportion and solve.

$$\frac{\text{Number who exercise daily}}{\text{total number of students}}$$

$$\frac{2}{5} = \frac{1036}{x}$$
$$2(x) = 5(1036)$$
$$\frac{2x}{2} = \frac{5180}{2}$$
$$x = 2590$$

Answer D

Reference: *Text.* Chapter 6, Section 6.9, Ratio and Proportion.

39. Replace b with - 3 and c with - 2.

$$a = 4bc^3$$
$$a = 4(-3)(-2)^3$$
$$y = 4(-3)(-8)$$
$$y = 96$$

Answer A

Reference: *Text*. Chapter1, Section 1.6, Evaluating Algebraic Expressions. There is more practice in the *Supplement*: Evaluating Algebraic Expressions -- Applied Problems. Also see the formulas for perimeter, circumference, area and volume inside the back cover of the text.

40. Let the unknown test score = x.

To find the average, add up the five scores, then divide by 5. Set you answer equal to 90, since this is the average we wish to attain.

$$\frac{65 + 100 + 90 + 95 + x}{5} = 90$$

$$\frac{350 + x}{5} = 90$$

$$350 + x = 450 \qquad \text{by cross multiplication}$$

$$x = 90$$

Answer A

Reference: *Supplement*. Whole Numbers, Finding the Average, Word Problems for Linear Equations With One Unknown.